About ASTD

American Society for Training and Development is the world's leading association of workplace learning and performance professionals, forming a world-class community of practice. ASTD's 70,000 members come from more than one hundred countries and 15,000 organizations, multinational corporations, medium-sized and small businesses, government, academia, consulting firms, and product and service suppliers.

Started in 1944 as the American Society of Training Directors, ASTD is now a global force, widening the industry's focus to connect learning and performance to measurable results, and is a sought-after voice on critical public policy issues.

For more information, visit www.astd.org or call 800.628.2783 (International, 703.683.8100).

D1306401

Also by Roger Schank

Making Minds Less Well Educated Than Our Own

Designing World-Class e-Learning:
How IBM, GE, Harvard Business School, and Columbia
University Are Succeeding at e-Learning

Engines for Education

Dynamic Memory Revisited

Tell Me a Story: Narrative and Intelligence (Rethinking Theory)

Scripts, Plans, Goals, and Understanding:
An Inquiry into Human Knowledge Structures

Virtual Learning:
A Revolutionary Approach to Building a Highly Skilled Workforce

Coloring Outside the Lines:
Raising a Smarter Kid by Breaking All the Rules

The Cognitive Computer:
On Language, Learning, and Artificial Intelligence

The Connoisseur's Guide to the Mind:
How We Think, How We Learn,
and What It Means to Be Intelligent

Creative Attitude:
Learning to Ask and Answer the Right Questions

About This Book

Why is this topic important?

All too often trainers are faced with having to teach what someone higher up in the organization said they had to teach. The problem is that those giving the orders may not have a clue as to what one can teach or how one might go about teaching it.

Training is not simply a matter of telling trainees what someone said they should hear, or at least it shouldn't be. Trainers need perspective, perspective gained from learning theory but also perspective gained from actual experience.

This book contains the kinds of questions trainers need to ask themselves and others before they start to design training.

What can you achieve with this book?

A trainer can begin to understand where and how to draw the line when thinking about building new training. What does it mean to teach better communication? How can you teach people not to do something? How can you help trainees build their own stories? How can you make training fun without being silly? How can you know what simply cannot be taught? How do you properly reward training successes?

How is this book organized?

The book is a wide-ranging collection of stories. The author has had extensive experience in designing new kinds of training for a large variety of corporations and schools. These experiences have taught him valuable lessons. In this book he tells the stories of some of those experiences, relating the lessons he has learned along the way.

About Pfeiffer

Pfeiffer serves the professional development and hands-on resource needs of training and human resource practitioners and gives them products to do their jobs better. We deliver proven ideas and solutions from experts in HR development and HR management, and we offer effective and customizable tools to improve workplace performance. From novice to seasoned professional, Pfeiffer is the source you can trust to make yourself and your organization more successful.

Essential Knowledge Pfeiffer produces insightful, practical, and comprehensive materials on topics that matter the most to training and HR professionals. Our Essential Knowledge resources translate the expertise of seasoned professionals into practical, how-to guidance on critical workplace issues and problems. These resources are supported by case studies, worksheets, and job aids and are frequently supplemented with CD-ROMs, websites, and other means of making the content easier to read, understand, and use.

Essential Tools Pfeiffer's Essential Tools resources save time and expense by offering proven, ready-to-use materials—including exercises, activities, games, instruments, and assessments—for use during a training or team-learning event. These resources are frequently offered in looseleaf or CD-ROM format to facilitate copying and customization of the material.

Pfeiffer also recognizes the remarkable power of new technologies in expanding the reach and effectiveness of training. While e-hype has often created whizbang solutions in search of a problem, we are dedicated to bringing convenience and enhancements to proven training solutions. All our e-tools comply with rigorous functionality standards. The most appropriate technology wrapped around essential content yields the perfect solution for today's on-the-go trainers and human resource professionals.

Pfeiffer
www.pfeiffer.com

Essential resources for training and HR professionals

Lessons in Learning, e-Learning, and Training

Perspectives and Guidance for the Enlightened Trainer

Roger C. Schank

Pfeiffer
A Wiley Imprint
www.pfeiffer.com

Copyright © 2005 by John Wiley & Sons, Inc.
Published by Pfeiffer
An Imprint of Wiley
989 Market Street, San Francisco, CA94103-1741
www.pfeiffer.com

Linking People,
Learning & Performance

1640 King Street   Box 1443
Alexandria, VA 22313-2043   USA
Tel *800.628.2783*   *703.683.8100*
Fax *703.683.8103*
www.astd.org

No part of this publication may be reproduced, stored in a retrieval system, or transmitted in any form or by any means, electronic, mechanical, photocopying, recording, scanning, or otherwise, except as permitted under Section 107 or 108 of the 1976 United States Copyright Act, without either the prior written permission of the Publisher, or authorization through payment of the appropriate per-copy fee to the Copyright Clearance Center, Inc., 222 Rosewood Drive, Danvers, MA 01923, 978-750-8400, fax 978-646-8600, or on the web at www.copyright.com. Requests to the Publisher for permission should be addressed to the Permissions Department, John Wiley & Sons, Inc., 111 River Street, Hoboken, NJ 07030, 201-748-6011, fax 201-748-6008, e-mail: permcoordinator@wiley.com.

For additional copies/bulk purchases of this book in the U.S. please contact 800-274-4434.

Pfeiffer books and products are available through most bookstores. To contact Pfeiffer directly call our Customer Care Department within the U.S. at 800-274-4434, outside the U.S. at 317-572-3985 or fax 317-572-4002 or www.pfeiffer.com.

Pfeiffer also publishes its books in a variety of electronic formats. Some content that appears in print may not be available in electronic books.

ISBN: 0-7879-7666-0

Library of Congress Cataloging-in-Publication Data

Schank, Roger C.
Lessons in learning, e-learning, and training: perspectives and guidance for the enlightened trainer / Roger C. Schank.
p. cm.
Includes bibliographical references and index.
ISBN 0-7879-7666-0 (alk. paper)
1. Employees—Training of. 2. Employees—Training of—Computer-assisted instruction. 3. Organizational learning—Data processing. 4. Computer-assisted instruction. 5. Internet in education. I. Title.
HF5549.5.T7S32665 2005
658.3'124—dc22
2004022988

Acquiring Editor: Matthew Davis
Director of Development: Kathleen Dolan Davies
Developmental Editor: Leslie Stephen
Editor: Rebecca Taff
Senior Production Editor: Dawn Kilgore
Manufacturing Supervisor: Becky Carreno

Printed in the United States of America
Printing 10   9   8   7   6   5   4   3   2   1

Contents

Foreword   xi

Introduction   xvii

1. I Told You Not to Tell Me That   1
   The case for not "telling" in training—and some
   guidelines for doing it if you must

2. I Wanted to Learn But There Was No Money in It   20
   Thoughts on the relationship between learning goals and
   rewards—and how to design training that helps learners
   stay motivated

3. Teaching What Can't Be Taught   40
   The value of knowing what you cannot fix—and
   understanding how people really change and what the
   culture has to do with it

4. Knowing Isn't Doing   48
   The reasons most e-learning is so bad (and other
   training, for that matter)—and five questions to ask to
   begin to make it better

5. Enron Fixes Their Communication Problems   60
   Thoughts on when to just say no—like when your
   company asks for a training course

6. Sex and Chicken   81
   The role of nonconscious learning—and how to help
   adults do it

7. I Can't Remember Whether I Ate the Whole Thing   91
   *On the difference between event memory and procedural
   memory—and how practice has to figure in*

8. Sir, Step Away from the Fig Newton   110
   *How what happens in real life undoes training—
   and what to do about it*

9. Billy's Home Run   121
   *Storytelling insights—and how hearing, telling, and
   living stories makes for good training*

10. What's Doing?   140
    *The excuses for not doing doing-based training—
    and how to avoid them*

11. Pardon Me, I Must Have Misplaced My Stereotype   161
    *The pros and cons of stereotyping—and how to teach
    people to do it well*

12. Every Curriculum Tells a Story (Don't It?)   183
    *The problems with most curricula today—and how
    they inspire a different way to define the training
    designer's job*

13. And We'll Have Fun, Fun, Fun 'til Our Company   203
    Takes the e-Learning Away
    *Why most e-learning is boring, not fun—and real-world
    tips for making it more engaging*

14. I Disagree with the Question   224
    *The importance of getting the questions right—so the
    rest of your job is easy*

15. Corporate Dragons   240
    *Why most e-learning you are likely to encounter isn't
    very good—and how to recognize it*

16. Time for AI 258
*How AI might help when you have a problem that you
need a smart computer to do—like building story-based
training systems*

About the Author 281

Index 283

Pfeiffer Publications Guide 293

Foreword

Sources of Wisdom

What do a chef in Groivenbroich, Germany, a man who wants to have a child but not a wife, and an aging athlete who passes up a homerun have to do with training? You will have to read this book to find out. You see, this is a book of stories as well as a book about how to use stories as instructional tools. The basic premise of this book is that learning is an inductive process. In everyday words, learning occurs by experience, and the best instruction offers learners opportunities to distill their knowledge and skills from interactive stories in the form of goal-based scenarios, team projects, and stories from experts.

As it happened, just as I was reading this book, I was sent a research review written by a team of research instructional psychologists titled: "Why minimally guided learning does not work: An analysis of the failure of constructivist, discovery, problem-based, experiential, and inquiry-based learning." This paper had no stories and was not as much fun to read as this book. However, it caught my attention because the main thesis of this paper is that inductive learning of the type described in this book is not a productive instructional strategy. As an alternative, the research paper recommends direct forms of instruction in which learners are provided or shown guidelines and steps followed by practice and feedback.

Who is right? How can practitioners integrate diverse and sometimes disparate sources of advice?

A related premise of this book—as well as many other books on training—is that telling does not lead to learning because learning requires doing. Training environments should emphasize active engagement with stories, cases, and projects. This seems intuitively right. We've all heard the expression that we learn 20 percent by listening, 30 percent by listening and looking, and 75 percent by *listening, looking,* and *doing*! However, consider a research study that came to quite opposite conclusions. Haidet and his colleagues (2004) randomly assigned two groups of medical residents to two different versions of a one-hour class on effective use of diagnostic tests. In the "active learning" version, the class was divided into small teams that worked on a series of problems related to the content. In between work sessions, the instructor discussed the concepts and issues generated by the group work. By working in teams to apply new knowledge to solve problems, this group pretty much applied the recommendations of this book. In the "teaching by telling" group, the instructor lectured from slides for an hour. Learning of both groups was measured with an assessment of knowledge and attitudes toward the content before the training, immediately after the training, and one month later. Learners also completed a reaction survey in which they evaluated the quality of their instructional environment. The results? Learners in both the active and passive sessions demonstrated significant gains and retention of knowledge. But there were no differences in learning between the two groups. Those in the didactic lecture group learned as much as those in the team-problem-solving group. Unexpectedly, the learners in the active session gave their session lower ratings of its value and its ability to meet learning objectives, even though they achieved the same learning as the passive group.

In spite of common wisdom that learning occurs by doing, in this study we see that learning was the same in a passive as in an active instructional environment. Who is right? How can practitioners integrate diverse sources of wisdom? As it happens, both sources of wisdom—the stories in this book and the research results—are right. To make sense of these conflicting results, we need to take a deeper look at what it means to learn by doing. There are actually at least three different forms of doing, all of which can, with the right learners, lead to learning. It turns out that individuals who have quite a bit of related background are able to process new information quite effectively, even when it's delivered in a passive format like a lecture. That is because they have already built mental models in memory that can guide their learning processes. Novice learners, however, need much more structure in their instruction and will usually benefit from overt opportunities to practice during training. In fact, learners who are very new to the knowledge and skills in the class are likely to learn most from a traditional, directive instructional environment that starts with show and tell of new skills followed by practice of those skills with feedback. More experienced learners are better equipped to profit from experiential environments like the ones recommended in this book. It is true that learners must process new content to learn. But some, like medical residents, can do that processing on their own; others need instructional guidance that leads them to overt practice opportunities.

It turns out that there are few universal rules for the "best" path to learning. Much depends on the knowledge and skills to be gained as well as the background experience of the learners.

What works well for experienced learners, like the medical residents in the research study, won't work as well for novices. Instructional techniques that work well to teach procedural skills like computer software training may not be as effective for more ill-defined outcomes such as sales or management.

Stories as Sources of Wisdom

And what about stories? As you read this book, you may feel a bit inadequate because you know you won't be able to create such engaging stories as the ones you read here. Fortunately, you can still use stories successfully. Stories support learning in one of two ways: by analogy or by springboards. Most of the stories in this book, as well as the stories we learned as children such as "The Tortoise and the Hare," are designed as analogies. Wisdom is embedded in the story itself. But you don't have to use creative stories to impart wisdom. A great deal of research points to the value of more mundane stories known as "worked examples." Basically, a worked example illustrates how to apply new steps or guidelines to complete a task. In that way a worked example provides a close analogy to what the learner will need to do as they acquire new skills. Stories like the ones in this book also serve as analogies. These stories provide more far analogies because their cover stories are often quite distant from the principles drawn from them.

Other types of stories serve as springboards to learning. These stories don't contain any wisdom, but they are used to provide the learner with a context for learning. Other names for these kinds of stories are case studies or problems. Springboard stories can be used at the beginning of an instructional program to focus learning as well as at the end of a program as a context for applying new skills. As we mentioned above, it is risky to use springboard stories that require novice learners to solve a problem at the same time that they are learning a new skill because it overloads their memory systems.

A Guide to the Book

To give you an overview of this book and to guide you to some of its themes is antithetical to the author's intention. Rather than telling you, at least telling you right away, the author uses stories as sources of wisdom. Following the stories, the author derives guidelines related to learning and instruction. So rather than disrupt this scheme with a summary, I'll make a few suggestions for ways you can get the most from this book.

1. *Enjoy the stories.* Some are funny, some are irreverent, and all are engaging. Many will leave you thinking.
2. *Compare the guidelines from these stories to other sources of wisdom, be it research evidence or your own experience.* Where they disagree, look under the surface to find out why. Often it's a matter of deciding which guidelines fit specific learning situations, since there are few absolute rules in training and instruction.
3. *Grab the nuggets of wisdom embedded in many of these chapters.* Consider how and when they might fit your instructional environments.
4. *Discuss the stories and their guidelines with others.* Stories are often open-ended enough to arouse multiple interpretations, and you can benefit from the insights of others who may learn different lessons from the stories than you learn.

5. *As you read the stories—most of them quite personal—ask yourself what the stories tell you about the author.* What are his assumptions and his values about himself, about life and learning? Take a minute to think about the stories that you tell and what they reveal about yourself.

6. *Decide which stories are your favorites and ask yourself why.* Is it because they are engaging? Is it because they resonate to your own experiences or assumptions about learning? Or is it because they made you think?

REFERENCE

Haidet, P., Richards, B.F., Morgan, R.O., Wrister, K., & Moran, B.J. (2004). A controlled trial of active versus passive learning strategies in a large group setting. *Advances in Health Sciences Education, 9,* 15–27.

Ruth Clark
Clark Training & Consulting
October 2004

Introduction

Getting the Most from This Resource

PURPOSE.   Trainers need to sit back and think a while before tackling a new project. They cannot simply blindly attempt to deliver what was asked for. Often those doing the asking do not know how to ask. Just telling trainees what some executive said they should know will not make for memorable training. This book is intended to supply trainers with ammunition to help them think about what is needed and confront those who ask for stuff that makes no sense.

AUDIENCE.   This book is meant for anyone who is ever called upon to design or deliver training. It is meant for people in e-learning and those in stand-up. It is meant for trainers and educators in general.

PRODUCT DESCRIPTION.   This is a collection of stories, lessons to be learned from those stories, and tips, guidelines, do's and don'ts, and other practical advice that follow from those lessons.

All together, these resources make up a virtual coaching session with a world-renowned thought leader, giving readers a chance to hear his often iconoclastic and always provocative insights and to get an inside track on profiting from his experience.

1

I Told You
Not to Tell Me That

THE CASE FOR NOT "TELLING" IN TRAINING—
AND SOME GUIDELINES FOR DOING IT IF YOU MUST

It often seems that everybody talks and nobody listens. We have come to think that the fault lies with the listener. But, I fear, the truth is quite different.

One of my favorite examples of talking without listening is in the song "Alice's Restaurant" (if you can call it a song—it goes on for twenty odd minutes). In it Arlo Guthrie tells the story of his arrest for littering and its subsequent effect when he appears for a physical examination in order to be drafted.

Throughout the song, no one is listening to anyone. Arlo tells his story, but the listeners don't want to hear it. My favorite part is when the induction sergeant speaks for forty-five minutes about how to fill in a form, but no one listens to a word that he says.

This kind of rambling speech about what to do before you do it is so common that it hardly seems worthy of mention. The airlines do it all the time (usually in multiple languages), especially when you are about to land in the United States from overseas and they want desperately to tell you how to fill in the immigration form.

The problem is, of course, that listening attentively will not actually help you fill out that form, no matter how many languages you hear it in. You can't remember what people tell you all that easily, especially when it comes in an unbroken soliloquy. As we will see in Chapter 7, you can't even remember fun stuff that happened to you all that well.

In the mind of every speaker, and every trainer, and especially every designer of training, is the idea that there is something he or she would like people to know. But . . .

Why Would Someone Want to Know What You Want to Teach?

I once asked this question of someone who was compiling a set of stories about her area of expertise to provide to her clients. She called to talk to me about storytelling and she mentioned her project. I asked her why anyone would want to hear the stories she had compiled. Why would they be listening to them? What would motivate them to do that? And what would they learn from them? She said these were very good questions.

Rather obvious questions if you ask me.

Oddly, the most obvious question—*Why would anyone want to know this?*—does not seem to be so obvious to most folks who design training.

> *Some very good (if obvious) questions*
> - Why would anyone want to hear the stories I have to tell?
> - Why would they be listening to them?
> - What would motivate them to do that?
> - What would they learn from them?
> - Why would anyone want to know this?

We are so used to having to learn subjects in which we have no interest at all that we simply assume that's what education ought to be. Curiously, this is never what self-directed education is. People who learn on their own learn exactly what they find interesting or potentially useful. I assume there are those who memorize Latin declensions because they think it is good for them, but they are in the minority.

> *People who learn on their own learn exactly what they find interesting or potentially useful.*

So, while we know better when we teach ourselves, when others teach, direct, or inform us we sit still for the boring and irrelevant. And, it follows, since designers of training know that students will sit still for whatever is thrown at them, we design training without thinking about what the student will be thinking when he or she is subjected to whatever it is we think he or she should know.

WANT AN EXAMPLE?

I once examined the e-learning products of a large publishing company. They had acquired them by buying a smaller company and asked me to see whether what they had acquired was worth anything. In the set of products I reviewed was one called *Handling Customer Complaints.*

The course begins with an exercise in which learners identify their attitudes toward complaints. The instruction begins with a voice-over explaining why complaints should be taken seriously, the percentage of people who complain, results of studies regarding customer complaints, and so on.

Presumably, the people who take this course are people whose job includes handling customer complaints. Would their job also include knowing the percentage of people who complain? How would knowing that, say, 23 percent of all customers complain help them handle complaints? Training is often full of information. It is as if information is somehow holy and needs to be known apart from its use. But information that is not used is forgotten, so why bother?

> *We design training without thinking about what the student will be thinking when he or she is subjected to whatever it is you think he or she should know.*

Later on in this course, learners view a hotel clerk who must help a guest with a problem. Learners do not have to help him solve the problem. Instead, they listen to the instructor talk through the steps people should follow when solving customer complaints.

At first glance this seems okay. There are a given number of steps in handling a complaint, so someone who is learning to handle complaints should learn those steps. Or should he? This is, of course . . .

The Heart of the Problem

I call this problem LIBITI—

Learn it because I thought it!

The LIBITI problem is hardly unique to trainers, of course. In fact, trainers would never even have thought to use LIBITI if it hadn't been used on them. Where? In school of course.

Consider Euclidean geometry for example. Euclid thought it up and students thousands of years later are proving isosceles triangles to be congruent. Of course, much lip service is paid to why it is good for the soul to know how to do such proofs, and no doubt there must be some value in it, but having every student in the world learn to do it seems just a little extreme. Why then do all students learn it? We learn it because someone important thought it up.

You have to agree that Euclidean proofs don't come up much in life. We tend to justify learning such things because we imagine that scholars have determined that the thoughts of great thinkers ought to be learned. Whether or not this is true, it has nevertheless left us with the idea that theories of things ought to be taught to practitioners of those things. We think that if you are going to become a carpenter, for example, that geometry might be especially useful, so we justify learning it because it might come up some day. The reality is that if we were really concerned with carpentry we would teach geometry in the context of carpentry, not worrying about proofs so much as worrying about getting the measurements right for something students were actually building.

> *LIBITI (learn it because I thought it) leaves us with the
> idea that theories of things ought to be taught to practi-
> tioners of those things.*

Trainers, however, seem to forget that LIBITI is really annoying to a student. So they present so and so's theory of customer service as a prelude to learning to do customer service, as if one were required for the other.

The motto of school? Theory first and then practice . . . although we don't always do the practice. Geometric proofs first and then carpentry, although most students never get to the carpentry. Physics first and then the use of materials, although most people never actually see any real materials. Biology first and then nutrition and health decisions, although . . . well, you get the idea.

As absurd as it is in school, *LIBITI is downright crazy in corporate training*. What is worse, not only don't your students care about the theory of customer complaint handling, they won't remember what was told to them anyway.

So, my simple message is:

don't tell anybody anything ever

Now I realize that simple messages are often quite difficult to understand, and typically statements like the one above are naturally disbelieved, since they seem so out of whack with everything that we have always understood to be true. What do you mean, never tell anyone anything? Not even the time of day if they ask? No, answering questions with short to-the-point answers is often okay to do, and so is helping someone out when she is stuck (sometimes), but you see once I add codicils it gets harder to know what I meant.

So, in that spirit, the rest of this chapter consists of me telling you something you may not need to or want to know—which violates my very point about not telling anybody anything ever.

Nevertheless here are . . .

Some Simple Principles About Telling in the Context of Training

Principle #1: Just-in-time information delivery makes information useful. . . OR, don't tell people things that they cannot immediately make use of

Don't tell anybody anything that he or she cannot immediately use. People forget what you tell them unless they can put it into immediate use. Even then, they will forget it unless you let them practice what they have learned a large number of times. If there is something you are just dying to tell them, bear in mind that you must tell them how to use that information and allow them to use that information immediately. Telling them how many people call up to complain is useless. What can they do with that?

Principle #2: Authentic activities motivate learners . . . OR, don't tell people how to do something they will never have to actually do in real life

So much of what passes as learning asks people to do something they would never actually have to do in their real lives. This sounds (and is) okay some of the time, particularly with kids. You need to be especially careful with adults however.

> *If I can identify someone who is acting defensive, does that help me to be less defensive? Will identifying a mistake make me less likely to do it myself?*

One e-learning course I looked at for the aforementioned publishing company had students match what characters they saw on the screen said with categories of the kinds of things that were bad to say (such as *making excuses* or *getting defensive*) in a given situation that people were being trained to handle. Now think about this for a second. What were the students learning? They were learning category names for bad behavior. Actually they were going to forget those soon enough. What they were doing was playing a matching game that had nothing to do with anything they would ever do in real life. Did the designers of this software think that learning to identify someone who was defensive in a cartoon would help students not to actually be defensive? If I have a problem with anger, will seeing someone else who is angry and saying "He is angry" help me be less angry?

ANOTHER EXAMPLE   *The course was attempting to teach people to send effective e-mails. The software had you identify mistakes in e-mails (like forgetting to send an attachment). Will being able to identify this mistake make you less likely to make it yourself? If you became a good identifier of what are pretty subtle e-mail mistakes as it turns out, would you suddenly become good at e-mail yourself? Why not let students just practice sending e-mails?*

Principle #3: Guessing is not doing. . . OR, don't make me guess the right answer you were dying to tell me

Remember the TV show *Let's Make a Deal?* Contestants were constantly having to choose to take what was behind door number 3 when they had no idea at all what they were choosing. A lot of e-learning and training programs are like that. We think nothing of asking trainees if they would take this course of action or that course of action. What happens when they are asked such questions goes something like this:

1. Figure out as best you can what the people who designed the program want you to choose.
2. Play out in your mind what might happen if you choose that course of action.
3. Look at all the other choices.
4. See which course of action might work out best.

Now . . . *compare this to the process that happens in real life when a course of action needs to be chosen:*

- Think up something to do.
- Do it.

In real life, you can't go down a list of alternatives and choose the best one. (Of course, there are exceptions—great chess players do exactly that. They think of all the moves they could make and try to play out as many consequences of those moves as they can and select the one that has the best outcome as far as they can figure. But those are chess players.) In real life we haven't the time or the ability to do that. We just react and later may wish that we had reacted better.

It is in this latter recapitulation of events where learning can take place. If we think about what we have done, and if we have some help, we can sometimes come to different conclusions about what we might have done. This may or may not help us to actually do things differently next time. Thinking isn't acting, after all.

But what we cannot do is list all the possible moves and then choose among them, unless we have a lot more time than we typically have.

So any training program that lets us choose from a list of alternatives is usually just playing a trick on us. That program is going to let us guess a right answer and then it is going to tell us what we should have done. This is just telling in a rather convoluted form. Don't just tell him right away, make him flounder around a little bit, convince him he really is making a choice, and then tell him. This is not a real breakthrough in the telling game.

> *In real life, you can't go down a list of alternatives and choose the best one. Any training program that lets us choose from alternatives is usually just playing a trick on us.*

Principle #4: Identification is not recall . . . OR, it doesn't really matter what you can show that you know

Ask any American if Idaho is a state and they will look at you as if you are nuts. Ask any American to name all fifty states and he or she won't be able to do it. They quite often leave out Idaho (and Utah and Delaware and so on). They can recognize them as states, but they can't recall them when needed.

A lot of knowledge is like that. We know it but we don't know it. It is on the tip of our tongues, we just knew it only a minute ago, but yet it's not there. Knowledge that doesn't come to mind each and every time we need it is really a different kind of stuff. It is often the names of things, words, memories, and such. It is not the kind of knowledge that we use regularly. We don't suddenly forget how to prepare the same breakfast we eat every morning nor do we forget how to start our cars. Nor do we suddenly become incapable of knowing that Idaho is a state.

Recognition knowledge and procedural knowledge—that is, knowledge we constantly use (we are always comprehending things and doing things)—never die. We use it and we don't lose it.

Recall knowledge—the stuff that tests are made of—is easy to forget, which is why people cram for tests. They are just trying to keep that stuff in their heads for a couple of hours.

> *If you can't recall it when you need it, you don't really know it . . .*

So it is ironic that the multiple-choice test was created. Multiple-choice tests test recognition knowledge. You don't have to remember anything; you just have to recognize an answer when you see it. For some people this is as good as cheating. They don't actually have to know anything; they just have to compare answers and figure out which is the best one. For others this is a nightmare, as all the answers look good to them and they are left figuring out the intentions of the test writer.

In either case, the test is meaningless. If you can't recall it when you need it, you don't really know it, or at least you don't know it in the form in which you would need to be able to use it.

Save your breath. If you are asking learners to choose from alternatives, you are simply asking them to do something that bears no relation to anything they will ever have to do in real life, so you may as well not bother. You can cram all you want for a test, but you won't be able to pass that same test as time goes by.

> *If you ask learners to choose from alternatives, you are asking them to do something that bears no relation to anything they will ever have to do in real life—so you may as well not bother.*

Principle #5: Playing a role has nothing to do with watching . . . OR, have somebody do something

I used to think that since people learn by doing, the best way to help them learn is to build a simulation and have them play a role that causes them to do some things that would be quite like what they might have to do in real life. Practicing in a simulation, as we learn from the air flight simulator, is a lot better than practicing on the real thing a lot of the time.

But I have found that life plays tricks on you when you say stuff that is obviously right but also is obviously hard. Simulations are hard to build, but lots of folks in the training world have heard me (and others) say how important they are to build. So now there is e-learning that uses simulations in which you don't play a role at all. Instead you watch someone else play a role and say what he or she should have done. These are, of course, much cheaper to build, since you don't have to build software that accounts for anything anyone might actually choose to do. There are no surprises.

> AHA! *Some simulations = multiple-choice tests + feedback on what you should have done = another form of telling!*

But yet again, we have a disguised version of a multiple-choice test with feedback on what you should have said or done, which is itself a disguised version of telling someone what the right answer is.

People just can't resist telling, can they?

Principle #6: Practice makes perfect . . . OR, if you teach it, have them do it one more time

If there were one word that you could remember after reading this book—I mean, memory is pretty flaky: you won't remember all that you read here—it would be

practice

It's a simple idea really. Music teachers and students show that they understand it when they play the same tune over and over again. Football players and coaches show that they understand it when they run the same plays over and over again. Feedback on what you should have said or done is a disguised version of practice.

Professionals show that they understand it when they actually refer to what they do as their *medical practice* or they use the term *the practice of law*.

But what about school? When is practice time? Is it when you have to do a hundred math examples? Yes, that is practice. Is it when you have to do a writing assignment. Yes, that's it too. What about when you are researching a paper or preparing a presentation? Those are a form of practice as well.

> *What is it that students spend the most time practicing throughout their school years?*

School does indeed use the concept of practice quite often. This is not to say that school uses that concept very well, however. What is it that students spend the most time practicing throughout their school years?

Test taking.

But as you might guess, practicing test taking gets you to be much better at test taking. Unfortunately, test taking doesn't come up all that much in an adult's life. So there is a lot of practice for a performance that never happens.

Now . . . what about your training?

What do learners in your organization practice when they are being trained? Recall when answering this, that practice does not mean trying something once. It means endless repetition, improving your performance with each try.

> *Practice means endless repetition, not just trying something once.*

> One aspect of the very nature of training also differentiates it from school: Each employee actually does practice something (his job) on a regular basis. Therefore, training should naturally lead into that practice. If the training isn't stuff that then gets reinforced by the job itself, something is really wrong with the training.

I have seen a lot of training that has nothing whatever to do with practice. Training that sets up practice is only valuable if the trainee gets to practice at the end. But training that has employees playing a game is only valuable if you are training them to play that game. Training that has employees memorize information is only valuable if you are training them to memorize information. Training that entails a teacher talking and a class listening is training people to sit quietly and listen.

No practice, no learning. It is pleasant to think otherwise, to rationalize everything that you do that isn't practice, to believe in the gods of transfer. As they say in my home town: *fuggedaboudit*.

I realize that you might be dying to ask me a question after reading all this. Since this is a book, you can't, but I can anticipate the question:

> *Why are you telling me all this stuff when*
> *the whole chapter is about how telling doesn't work?*

Right.

Good question.

So here is what to do. Close the book immediately after I tell you. Then write down the six principles you just read.

Okay.

Now.

Close the book. When you give up, open it again.

I bet you can't do it, can you? Yes, I am sure you remember some of them. You just read them, after all. Even if you remembered them all, how many do you think you will remember next week? Next year?

"So, why read all this stuff?" you are asking. "And why does he bother to write it?" you are wondering.

I am not operating under the illusion that you will remember what I have written. It hardly matters. You probably don't agree with half of it anyway.

What I am hoping is that I am causing you think about what you are doing while you are reading—that you are relating what I am saying to your own experiences.

> ***My hope for this book . . .*** *that by reading these essays you are starting to reflect on what you are doing in training or might plan to do in training.*

In other words you are starting to reflect on what you are doing in training or might plan to do in training. You may wake up in the middle of the night with an idea that I helped jump start with what you read. That would be my goal. Remembering what I said is not my goal. Nor should it be yours.

Can you do this in training? Yes, you can. You can make people reflect on what they do by engaging them in the reflection process.

This leads to my last observation:

Principle #7: Make people reflect . . . AND, get a dialogue started

How do you get people to think about what they do and why is it a worthwhile exercise?

Recall that it is my view that people learn only by doing. One form of doing is conversation. Conversation with others or with oneself can cause one to mentally practice. Mental practice is pretty good stuff. Not everything is about hitting keys or running pass formations. Some practice is just thinking about what one does and then re-thinking. Dreaming tends to be about this. We rehearse what we have done or think we will do under various conditions. Dreams haunt us when we feel we have not done things quite right. Daydreaming is like this as well. We imagine circumstances and think about what we might say or do.

> *One form of doing is conversation. Conversation with others or with yourself is a form of mental practice.*

This kind of thing should not solely be left to chance. Training should entail a serious effort to get employees to reflect on what they do and to examine ways that they can do better. By this I do not mean chastising them for mistakes. Enable employees to teach themselves about what they do.

Socrates believed that all knowledge was already inside a person and simply needed to be drawn out. While no one believes this today, the Socratic method of teaching has proven to be quite useful in getting people to come to their own conclusions—to think about ideas rather than listen to ideas.

Be a Socratic trainer. Draw out from trainees what is inside them. Make them teach themselves. And don't tell anybody anything.

◊　◊　◊

Jump Start Your Training

How to be a Socratic trainer? Try acting less like a teacher and more like a mentor. Some advice:

Be ignorant

When asked, a good mentor claims ignorance. Your favorite response to a learner's question should be: *I really don't know. What do you think?*

Let people be themselves

Not every trainee will be good at what you are trying to teach. If they can't do it, let them alone.

Know when to tell and when to be quiet

You can tell people the answer when the answer is a small missing fact that would mean having to spend inordinate amounts of time attempting to figure it out on their own. You can tell an employee the answer when following the wrong course of action might lead to danger or a recovery period that is way too long given the situation.

Don't tell anyone anything if you know they can figure it out on their own.

Make suggestions

The real role of a mentor is to make suggestions. Of course, there are suggestions and there are suggestions. When suggestions look like the gospel, they are bad. When they are presented as something to think about, they are good.

When an employee is spinning his wheels and accomplishing nothing, put him on a solid footing and let him start again. A mentor needs to recognize when just-in-time help will really help and not be a crutch. This is the essence of the art of mentoring.

Lie to your trainees

Say things you don't believe if it will advance the cause of the students thinking harder about how to defeat you. It is not your job to show the trainees how smart you are nor to earn the trainees' respect for your good ideas. It is much better to make the trainees think hard.

Know when to hand hold

Holding learners' hands while they attempt to do something can be very tempting. It is possible to hold trainees' hands too much, to have them follow your lead and seem to understand, only to find out that, when left to their own devices, they cannot do it on their own. Know when to let go.

Practice, practice, practice

Practice is the essence of doing correctly. Good mentors know when more practice is needed. Good mentors also know when the rest of what is to be done can be skipped because the learner got it faster than expected. If what you are teaching can't be practiced, stop teaching it.

2

I Wanted to Learn,
But There Was
No Money in It

THOUGHTS ON THE RELATIONSHIP BETWEEN
LEARNING GOALS AND REWARDS—AND HOW TO DESIGN
TRAINING THAT HELPS LEARNERS STAY MOTIVATED

When I first moved to Chicago, the local press made a big fuss about it and consequently every civic group that was trying to fix education suddenly wanted me to be part of their group. One meeting I attended, held at 7:30 a.m., which pretty much made it the last meeting of that group I attended, was dominated by a civic leader who had a proposal to fix the inner city schools. His plan was to pay children for grades. He was offering $5 for a C, $10 for a B, and $15 for an A.

No. Really. This was a serious proposal.

I didn't know where to start in explaining education to someone who means well but was this clueless. Obviously, he thought the kids would work harder if there was a reward. Clearly he believed that the reward system in school was broken. In this he was quite right. If he had really looked at this issue from the kids' point of view, he might have realized that his proposal was tantamount to thinking that kids *want* to learn, but since there isn't any money in it, they don't bother. Cute, but misguided. There has probably never been a child who has expressed such a thought—which would more or less guarantee that this was a solution in search of the problem it was trying to solve.

If the reward system is screwed up in education, it does indeed need to be fixed, but it should be fixed within the boundaries of the needs of the student. For kids this doesn't mean giving them candy instead of money. It means giving them education that satisfies some goals that they have or honestly believe they are likely to have. When a kid doesn't learn algebra and explains it away with the "I am never going to need that stuff" excuse, we must realize that the kid knows what he is talking about. Algebra, as Peggy Sue says in *Peggy Sue Got Married*, simply doesn't come up later in life.

The simple fact is the kid doesn't learn because he doesn't believe in the reward system that has been put in front of him, which says: learn this and it will be good for you later. He can be motivated by such promises, but he must believe in them first.

Of course, this is all true in training as well . . . yet trainees quite often do want to do well in a training course. One is prone to wonder why.

Here are some reasons . . .

Why Trainees Might Want to Do Well in a Training Course

See which ones best fit your experience:

1. They are used to school, training looks like school, so they go back to old habits.

2. They want to show their fellow employees how smart they are.

3. They believe that superiors are watching and that they will know who did well and be impressed.

4. They really get into hard problems.

5. They believe that what they will learn will help them do a better job at work.

6. The training is the local currency of conversation, like this week's hot movie, and not being able to discuss it leaves you out of it at work.

7. The trainees have been dying to learn how to do something and the training teaches just what they have always wanted to know.

8. Doing well at the training qualifies them for the next step at work.

9. The training is being held in a really good vacation-like spot and they want to be sure they get to come back next year.

10. The training is a lot of fun, and the better you do the more fun it is.

And the correct answer is . . .

There is a correct answer, of course. But it is not an answer that is all that obvious, so we need to think about what we are trying to accomplish in training first. Then maybe we can understand how rewards actually work.

The best way to understand how rewards really work
in education is to look at how and why we learn anything.

Let's start early. Why do we learn to walk and talk?

It seems fairly obvious that walking is a good idea. It is much easier than crawling, a fact that every child learns sooner or later. But why try to get around at all? Why not just lie around all day and wait for stuff to come to you? Although some have tried this, I suppose, the answer is simple enough. Sometimes there are objects we want that are not near us, or people whom we want to be near who don't seem to want to move to us, or there are things we can only do in a location different from the one we are in. So we figure out how to get around.

Note that we don't learn to walk because it feels good to do so, although it does; or because we want to please our parents, although it will; or because we are in a competition with other babies; or we are hoping for some external reward. Any or all of these factors may be present even in learning to walk. In other words we can go where we want to go. It is the satisfaction in the accomplishment and the benefits that continue to accrue to us as a result of our newly learned skill that cause us to learn to walk and to practice that skill every day of our lives.

> *The real reason we try and try again to learn anything*
> *is that we can execute our own independent desires.*

The same is true of talking, of course. Talking is its own reward. It is an incredibly arduous task to learn a language. Nevertheless, everyone learns one. One does this initially because it is easier to get a cookie if you say "cookie" than if you cry. We get more sophisticated in our language use because we recognize the power of language. Every new word, every new way of expressing an idea, that helps us communicate our thoughts better seems to be rewarded by how others react to us. We feel understood; we get what we want; we are approved of for being interesting; or thought provoking; or novel; or funny. When others listen, we feel powerful. Language skills, like locomotion skills, provide independence and make us feel good about the control we have over our own world.

The aspects of learning that are true when we learn to walk and talk are always true:

1. There is a goal that learning the skill will help us achieve.

2. The accomplishment of that goal is the reward.

3. The approval of others is a vital element of the process, but is not sufficient to motivate learning.

4. After the skill has been tried and its first elements learned, the skill is practiced every day for the rest of one's life.

5. There is continuous improvement.

6. Apart from other goals, the skill enables independence.

7. The initial rewards are sufficient to motivate learning.

8. Rewards that accrue from this skill later on in life are unknown to the learner at the time of learning.

9. Failure is no problem. In fact, failure occurs with nearly every attempt.

10. The process itself is not fun, but neither is it terribly painful or annoying.

Remember, we are concerned with rewards here. So with that in mind, let's consider the kinds of rewards inherent in the trainees' top ten reasons for wanting to do well in a training course:

1. They are used to school, training looks like school, so they go back to old habits.

   HABIT

2. They want to show their fellow employees how smart they are.

   EGO

3. They believe that superiors are watching and that they will know who did well and be impressed.

   HOPE (external)

4. They really get into hard problems.

   PROBLEM SOLVING

5. They believe that what they will learn will help them do a better job at work.

   HOPE (internal)

6. The training is the local currency of conversation, like this week's hot movie, and not being able to discuss it leaves you out of it at work.

   COMMUNITY

7. The trainees have been dying to learn how to do something, and the training teaches just what they have always wanted to know.

   KNOWLEDGE

8. Doing well at the training qualifies them for the next step at work.

   QUALIFICATIONS

9. The training is being held in a really good vacation-like spot, and they want to be sure they get to come back next year.

EXTERNAL

10. The training is a lot of fun, and the better you do the more fun it is.

INTERNAL

The words I have placed under each sentence represent the type of reward represented by that sentence. These are . . .

THE TEN TYPICAL REWARDS FOUND IN ANY EDUCATIONAL SITUATION

Let's look at them more closely:

#1. Habit

Much of what we do in life we do out of habit. Doing things that are familiar can be an enjoyable experience. We listen to the same songs again and again, watch old movies, and generally reminisce about old experiences, even ones that were not so pleasant. School habits are ones we all acquired and practiced for many years. We know how to sit in a classroom and try to please the teacher. We accept training because HABIT is a kind of reward. The more familiar something is, the more internal memories of previous experiences guide our behavior and reward us with a sense of the familiar.

Some pointers: Use the HABIT reward at your own peril. You can expect that people will show up for training at a school-like environment and behave as they once did in school. But remember that not every student was successful at school and they will fall into old habits that may not be what you had in mind. Remember too, school was not using the HABIT reward; it used grades, parental pressure, and other external rewards to get anyone to pay attention, and these are not easily available in corporate training.

#2. Ego

Egotism can be a great motivator. People want others to see how smart they are, how clever they are, how good they are at whatever is being attempted. Schools have used the EGO reward as long as there have been schools. School is a competition. It shouldn't be, but it usually is. This is true at every level of schooling. Ph.D. students want to be seen as the best in their group for a good reason: they want the recommendation of the professor for the Harvard job. High school students want to graduate number one so they can go to Harvard. In general, these people don't know whether Harvard is really the be all and end all of existence. Maybe it is no fun at all to be at Harvard. But EGO demands its reward.

Some pointers: The EGO reward is rather out of place in the workplace. In school there is one victor (maybe a few more) who can go to Harvard, be valedictorian, and so on. In the workplace, if only one person considers himself a success at training this can be a real problem. When I went back to my twenty-fifth high school reunion, I discovered that even the guy who graduated number 5 in the class (of a very competitive smart kids' school) considered himself a failure. (I wasn't wildly proud of being number 322 either.) No employer can afford to have trainees feel like failures after training.

#3. Hope (External)

The EXTERNAL HOPE goal is really the most common reward used in education. If you do well good things will happen. No one is quite sure *what* good things will happen (or when). In fact, the less clearly stated these rewards are, the easier they are to dangle in front of students.

Some pointers: Corporations tend to be ambivalent about using this type of reward. They always say that the training is important, by which they mean that your success in the company depends on it, but there are too many examples of people who blow off training and yet do very well in the company. In fact, the realities of the workplace make this reward quite difficult to use. You could do it by linking success at training to pay raises and such, but that seems an odd thing to do, as performance on the job is always more important than performance in training. At school there is no job going on in parallel, so this reward works there, but it will not work when there really is a job that is always more important than the training itself.

#4. Problem Solving

There is great reward in a job well done, and there is great reward in solving a hard problem. People do crossword puzzles or tinker with car engines for just this reason. But relying on the PROBLEM SOLVING reward to motivate students is a tricky business. It works, but only when the problem is inherently fascinating, absorbing, and worthy of the time put into it.

Some pointers: This reward can really work well in corporate training, but you cannot simply assume that it will work in every instance. People are, after all, quite different from one another and what fascinates me may not fascinate you. Nevertheless, if a problem is well chosen, the PROBLEM SOLVING reward can work well both in school and in training.

#5. Hope (Internal)

The INTERNAL HOPE reward differs from the EXTERNAL HOPE reward only slightly, but it is worthy of comment. With HOPE as a type of internal reward, people really do want to do well at what they do and so they can try to learn something because they hope it will enable them to do better. But HOPE is not a wholly internal kind of reward. People want to do better, at least in part because they assume there will be some external reward as well.

Some pointers: You can use the INTERNAL HOPE reward in training, but be careful. It works only with people whose internal value system is unaffected by external rewards.

#6. Community

The COMMUNITY reward is one that depends on a strong social infrastructure at work. When people at work really talk with one another, it is very good for the company if they are talking about work. One way to make this happen is to make training a sociological experience. By that I mean having the training have such interesting things happening in it that people can't help but talk about it. In simulations we have built, we have created characters who were so annoying that the trainees who interacted with them couldn't help but talk about that experience with each other. This served to reinforce the training.

Some pointers: People will want to attend training if there is a COMMUNITY reward. The training they receive will be remembered if what they talk about had to do with what was going on in the training (and not some funny joke that the trainer told).

#7. Knowledge

KNOWLEDGE is its own reward, we hear. And sometimes it is. There are subjects that trainees really seriously want to learn about. In that case, just teach those to them and everything will be fine. (But bear in mind that telling is not teaching.)

Some pointers: Most of the time KNOWLEDGE is not its own reward. Think about school. Was algebra its own reward? Were French declensions their own reward? Maybe years later on your trip to Paris they came in handy (if you remembered them), but that is not the KNOWLEDGE for its own sake reward. Far too often, relying on KNOWLEDGE as a reward is a sure way to build really bad training.

#8. Qualifications

Because school has prerequisite courses that lead to other courses, we are quite used to having to take a course because it qualifies us for something else. But beware of using the QUAL-IFICATIONS reward in training. Just as they did in school, people will figure out what the minimum is and do that. Once you set up the QUALIFICATIONS reward, you also start having learners figuring out how to game the system. They figure what they can get away with and still get the qualification. When there is a qualifying test of some sort, they simply study for the test and typically can pass the test only for a brief moment before they forget everything they memorized.

Some pointers: The QUALIFICATIONS reward is often the antithesis of education and really has no place in training unless it is a physical skill you are teaching. In that case, seeing that you can drive the car (rather than passing a multiple-choice test) is a legitimate test of qualifications. So the ability to use a machine at work, say, would be a good way to make sure that someone is qualified for a job that uses that machine. But other than that sort of physical qualification, other types of qualifications are perceived by adult learners as being rather arbitrary and are not taken seriously.

#9. External

The EXTERNAL reward is, of course, where this chapter started. This is the pay for grades idea. Companies use external rewards as well. Of course, paying for success on the job is a real reward and trips to sunny climes for hard-working salespeople in Chicago work really well. But we are talking training here. EXTERNAL rewards don't really work in training.

Some pointers: You can't get someone to learn something because there is a nice trip in it for her if she does. Learning isn't like that. It requires practice, not one-time all-out pushes. The late-nighters you pulled in school don't really teach you much (except maybe that you can work well on uppers). What you learn without practice and reflection you soon forget.

#10. Internal

INTERNAL rewards are the best. We do anything well that we do because we really want to do it. Being motivated from inside is what makes anyone into a great competitor or an accomplished player in his field of choice.

Some pointers: The trick for trainers is to understand what the INTERNAL rewards are for their trainees. What makes them tick? What do they care about? I recall having a group of experienced employees sign up for training we had built for new hires. When we asked why, they said that there were some simulated customers in the systems we built that they had never dealt with in real life and they wanted to practice on them. Now those were employees with INTERNAL motivation. They wanted to be good at what they did because it made them feel more empowered.

> *The trick for trainers is to understand what the INTERNAL rewards are for their trainees. What makes them tick? What do they care about?*

The Short List

Here is the short list of rewards that can work in training if they have been handled properly:

PROBLEM SOLVING

COMMUNITY

To put this simply, when the problem a trainee is working on is its own reward, when solving it makes her feel good, the solution itself is its own reward.

When a group is working on something that gives them some common ground to talk about and reflect on, learning will happen. Thus, the building of community can serve as a reward in training.

The next three work only some of the time, and the circumstances have to be just right:

KNOWLEDGE

QUALIFICATIONS

INTERNAL

In order for these three to work, the trainee has to be of a certain mindset entering training. He has to be, in other words, self-motivated. These rewards are internal and thus, as a designer of training, you really can't do much to take advantage of these rewards. Designing training hoping that these rewards will kick in is probably a bad idea.

With this knowledge of how rewards work in hand, we are ready to look again at . . .

The Top Ten List of the Things That Are Typically True When Learning Takes Place Naturally

When learning is working, the following tend to be true:

1. There is a goal that learning the skill will help us achieve.

2. The accomplishment of that goal is the reward.

3. The approval of others is a vital element of the process but is not sufficient to motivate learning.

4. After the skill has been tried and its first elements

learned, the skill is practiced every day for the rest of one's life.

5. There is continuous improvement.

6. Apart from other goals, the skill enables independence.

7. The initial rewards are sufficient to motivate learning.

8. Rewards that accrue from this skill later on in life are unknown to the learner at the time of learning.

9. Failure is no problem. In fact, failure occurs with nearly every attempt.

10. The process itself is not fun, but neither is it terribly painful or annoying.

These are sufficient to use as *rules of thumb for the design of good training.*

Where Do the Rewards Come In?

Consider the five rewards that actually work in the light of this list of ten things that are true when learning takes place. When a group (COMMUNITY) is working together on a problem (PROBLEM SOLVING) that will give them KNOWLEDGE to be able to do something they couldn't do before (QUALIFICATIONS), they will learn a great deal if they are ready and eager to be part of the process (INTERNAL).

The rewards are naturally built into a well-designed learning process. Trainers should never concern themselves with building rewards into the training they provide. The training must provide its own rewards. But it is very easy to abuse this idea. We can't just assume that trainees come to training with the right rewards built in. Too many teachers assume that their students want to learn when that simply isn't the case. Students often will not want what you want them to want and thus will not be motivated. The solution then is to design training that is by its very nature inclusive of the naturally occurring learning goals and internal reward system. So the question is . . .

How Do You Do This?

> *The way to help learners be motivated is to design training that by its very nature incorporates the naturally occurring learning goals and internal reward system.*

Here are some tips to follow . . .

1. Make Sure Training Is a Group Process

Training cannot occur in isolation. Often we design group training because we see this as being an economical way of teaching. That may well be, but a larger advantage has to do with the reward system. Reflection is a large part of learning. We don't simply learn, we also discuss what we have learned and what we think about what we have learned. This reflection process is a kind of mental practice of ideas and is critical to the learning process. Students can most certainly take one-on-one training or work on one-on-one simulations. That is a great way to learn. But all the individuals who are learning that way must talk together at some point to reinforce what they learned. By this I do not mean running a discussion group. (The rewards in discussion groups are usually about egos, not learning.) I mean that after a solitary learning exercise a group exercise of some sort must follow.

The key idea here: practice, and practice not only includes practicing what to do but also includes practicing what to think. The latter requires others to bounce ideas off. This means that there really has to be something to discuss. Maybe the group has to make a decision or a plan of attack on the next problem. The discussions can't be perfunctory; they must be critical to success in the project. If that is the case, then the learning process will be enhanced by each discussion.

2. Make Sure Training Is a Problem-Solving Process

Those who know my utter contempt for the Tower of Hanoi and the Missionary and Cannibals problems as ways of teaching reasoning would be surprised at what I have just laid out as rule 2. But I am really not referring to that kind of problem solving. I am suggesting that a group that is working together in training to accomplish something will most certainly begin to see the accomplishment of their goal as an important internal reward and will take it quite seriously.

Whatever we work on for a long while takes on great value within the community that is working on it. A political campaign, for example, draws together the campaign workers in a commitment that often transcends the candidate and makes the team's devotion to getting the candidate elected more important than the candidate himself. Teams that work together to achieve a goal wind up motivating each individual member of the team and supplying the necessary rewards.

> *Teams that work together to achieve a goal wind up motivating each individual member of the team and supplying the necessary rewards.*

3. Make Sure That Whatever Is Learned Is Merely a Prelude

Learning in a vacuum causes immediate memory loss. No one remembers what she learned and then never used. Whatever the initial project that a team is working on, it must be part of an ongoing series of projects, each one building on the one before in order to cause real learning to take place. When a child learns to take a few steps he would quickly forget how he did it if he didn't keep trying to improve on the process for the next few years (or for the rest of his life really). Everything he learns is a part of a growth plan to learn more and get better.

Anything you learn in training must be continually practiced to be retained. This means that training that is not building on what was learned previously in training will not work. Schools try to achieve this with prerequisites and such, but usually prerequisites are for the convenience of the teacher so that they don't have to teach the basics again, and they quite often do not build upon nor do they reinforce what was learned earlier.

To put this simply: don't teach anything in a first course that will not be used in a subsequent (that is, immediately subsequent) course. This rule applies not only to courses, but to days, hours, and any other unit you can think of. If you teach it to me today, then make me practice it tomorrow.

4. Make Sure Independence Is in Sight

Groups and teams are fine, but someone who needs the team in order to function has not really learned what she needs to learn. You can't learn to talk without having someone to talk to, but eventually you really are on your own. Mom won't always be there to help you say what you mean. Similarly, every skill has to be (in principle) one that can be done independently, even if it was learned as part of a group process. A good training program helps trainees function on their own after functioning as part of a group during the training period.

◊　　◊　　◊

Jump Start Your Training

A few reminders:

External Rewards Have No Place in Training

You can have your trainees compete for prizes and those who win will certainly remember (and presumably enjoy) winning. But they will not remember what they learned that helped them win. There is many a valedictorian who couldn't pass a single test he aced two years after he graduated.

Internal Rewards Work Best

If you can get at what people really want to be able to do, they will be right there with you during the training. People always want to be able to work well with others, the experience itself is rewarding, and they love being able to solve a hard problem with only a little help.

Use Knowledge and Qualifications as Rewards Cautiously

Gaining knowledge or new qualifications can be rewarding, but only if it is clear to the learner that the new knowledge is of value and that the new qualifications will be recognized by the company. Make sure that employees see the value of what they have learned if the value is not internal.

Let Go

Adults, like children, know when they are capable of standing on their own two feet. Let them fall. They will get up soon enough if they know they can.

3

Teaching
What Can't Be Taught

THE VALUE OF KNOWING WHAT YOU CANNOT FIX—
AND UNDERSTANDING HOW PEOPLE REALLY CHANGE
AND WHAT THE COMPANY CULTURE HAS TO DO WITH IT

I once was asked to build a training program for a very large company on sexual harassment. (They were against it.) The manager of this project was an attractive young woman whom I got to know as the project progressed. After a while she told me that she was being sexually harassed on a regular basis by her boss and by her boss's boss. It got so bad she was afraid to go into work in the morning. She was certain she would never be promoted as long as she kept rebuffing them.

Of course, it was they who were sponsoring the training program.

The whole idea of building a sexual harassment training program is just a little troublesome, to say the least. We can build simulated characters with whom a trainee can interact, but what will the issue in the program be? Will we present women to the user and ask them if they would like to make annoying comments or not? Who is likely to harass a cartoon?

What we did do was have trainees play the role of managers who were confronted with situations with which their employees were involved—one sent a pornographic picture to another, for example—and ask them what they should do about it. But this was just an exercise in knowing the law. Trainees needed to know what was considered harassment and what was not. Was a comment on a woman's clothing okay? How about her figure?

The exercise left me cold. I helped design the program, but I doubted it would mean much. My colleague continued to get harassed throughout the software development phase . . . and afterwards.

CAN YOU REALLY TEACH THIS KIND OF THING?

What does it mean to try and teach conceptual change or attitude adjustment? How can you teach this woman's bosses that they were making her life miserable?

We could record women's stories about being harassed and make men listen to them, but if that was all there was to it nothing would ever go bad in the world at all. We would just hear distressing stories and stop what we were doing. It really doesn't work like that. *Some things are just really hard to teach.* Attitude about oneself and the way one treats others are pretty much in there by the time your company has hired its people. Children can change as circumstances alter their perception of things. But for adults it is a whole lot harder.

So How *Do* People Change?

When my son was small, I coached his little league team. There was one kid on the team who was a head taller than my son and nearly everybody else. When he stuck his bat out, the ball went quite a ways. He didn't really swing properly. In fact, he hardly swung at all. He was just real strong. No matter what he did the ball went flying. I tried to teach him to hit properly, but he would have none of it. He goofed around, and nevertheless, things went well. He had such great ability that he could do no wrong. I wondered what would happen to him when the competition got tougher. He had nowhere near the desire and intensity that my son had, but he had three times the ability.

Later, I invited my son to bring his friends over for a little backyard tackle football. This kid played fullback. No one could tackle him. He simply bowled everyone over. None of what he did was done properly. Yet again he was uncoachable. He didn't know what he was doing, but he did it effectively. He saw no need to try harder or to learn to do things better.

Again I wondered what would become of him.

Some years later I found out. He was the star on defense on the Wisconsin football team. I watched him cause havoc when he played against Northwestern (where I worked at the time). Soon enough he was in the NFL.

It was hard to track him in the NFL. He certainly wasn't a star, and although he seems to have been in the NFL by 2001 he didn't seem to be playing any longer. Here is what I found on the Internet:

TAREK SALEH

Height: *6–0*

Weight: *240*

Born: *11/07/1974*

College: *Wisconsin [All American]*

NFL Experience: *6*

College Notes: *Four-year letterman and three-year starter. Played rush linebacker in a down position most of the time or as defensive end and was used as a pass rusher on almost all passing downs. Had 68 tackles, 20 tackles for a loss, and 14 sacks in 1996. Intense player and great competitor with non-stop work ethic. Plays every down. Quick and tough. Appears to be able to play linebacker in the NFL.*

Acquired: *1997 Draft, 4th Round #26 (#122 overall).*

1997, 1998: *Saleh was hoped to replace Kevin Greene at outside linebacker, but never lived up to expectations.*

1999: *Saleh was selected sixth by the Cleveland Browns in the 1999 Expansion Draft.*

5/10/99: *Coach Palmer reveals that the Browns have switched Saleh to fullback from linebacker. "He's 6–2 and 240. I think he'll go in and hit somebody. We're still looking for a blocking fullback. Carolina tried to do that with him last year."*

5/22/99: *Saleh says that he's happy with the switch from linebacker to fullback, a position he played in high school (and caused Syracuse to recruit him). "I like it a lot. I consider myself a fullback now. I think fullback is something I can excel at. Now I'm a big fullback. Before I was a small linebacker."*

7/28/99: Saleh plays a role in a nerve-racking event in training camp. Near the end of practice, Saleh slammed into Chris Spielman with enough force to nearly make Spielman unconscious. "It was a great hit," said Coach Palmer. "On a scale of one to 10, it was a 10."

10/15/99: Saleh has done a nice job on special teams this season, including recovering a fumble on a kick-return by Cincinatti in Week 5.

I often think of Tarek when I think about teaching intangibles. I thought he needed to be taught to try hard and I couldn't reach him. Of course he was only 8 or 9 at the time. But someone or something obviously did reach him. No, he didn't become an NFL star, but few do. He did learn to play hard, apparently. In fact, as a small linebacker who made it in the NFL he probably played above his ability.

So How Do People Learn to Want to Try Hard and Succeed?

What happened that taught Tarek that one thing that seems so unteachable and yet is so vitally important to any organization? Employees who really care to do well at their jobs, who really want to succeed, and who try their hardest—isn't that the real goal in any organization and therefore the real goal in training?

I have no idea.

But I have some guesses that might apply:

1. He found he couldn't get by on size alone and changed his attitude.

2. Some coach was really hard on him and convinced him to start trying.

3. He found someone to compete with who inspired him to beat him.

4. He found a role model to imitate.

5. Some disaster or near disaster occurred that changed his perspective.

6. He simply woke up one day.

Now, I have no idea if any of these things happened, and in fact, it simply doesn't matter for our purposes. *The point is that these are the kinds of things that turn people around.* When people experience attitude shifts, we don't ask them who taught them to have heart or to care or to adopt a different work ethic. We never ask about the teacher or the class they took or the school they went to that caused this kind of fundamental change. We don't ask this because we know that there could have been no such teacher or class or school.

> *Experiences make us wiser, not people and certainly not classes.*

It is events that cause change of this sort. Experiences make us wiser, not people and certainly not classes. To change from an uncoachable backyard fullback into a college All American and NFL success, Tarek had to have had some kind of internal awakening or some external event occur. Certainly a person, in the form of a coach or role model, might have had a great deal to do with it. But we know it just wasn't a class he took on attitude change that changed his attitude.

And what is the lesson here?

There Is a Lot of Stuff
You Simply Cannot Teach

You can, however, help to create an environment where not working your hardest simply does not cut it. We are talking about culture change and not about school or training. The very large company that permitted sexual harassment was led, not surprisingly, by a man who seemed to be constantly, and publicly, involved with various women, and whose divorce was national news. It really didn't matter what sexual harassment course they taught at this company. Everyone understood the prevailing culture. No trainer or training was going to change it.

It always is a good idea to know what you cannot fix and spend energy elsewhere.

◊   ◊   ◊

Jump Start Your Training

Think about Tarek when you think about needed attitude adjustment in your company and remember this:

Not everything is a training issue.

Think about what might have changed Tarek and see how you can make that kind of thing happen in your company. You may not be able to fix the corporate culture, but at least you can avoid wasting time building training that won't matter.

A FEW POINTERS

- Think hard about what can and cannot be taught.
- Find out before you start to build training whether

the company really cares about what you are asked to train employees to do.

- Recognize that you can't train employees to behave in ways that highers up don't behave.

- Learn to see which problems can actually be addressed by training, and which cannot.

- Figure out how to help create a "learning culture" where those who learn are rewarded and emulated.

And probably most important of all . . .

- Always try to have your training address what the organization really needs, not just what they ask for.

4

Knowing Isn't Doing

THE REASONS WHY MOST E-LEARNING
(AND OTHER TRAINING, FOR THAT MATTER) IS SO BAD—
AND FIVE QUESTIONS TO ASK TO BEGIN TO MAKE IT BETTER.

Everyone seems to want to do e-learning these days. They have all been told how to buy the right stuff to get started, and perhaps they are having fun trying to do it. Occasionally companies find they are not having fun, and when that happens sometimes they call me. People don't usually admit to being in over their heads, so it was rather strange to get a call about a company that had been building e-learning for a while but thought they were doing a bad job. I mean, who ever thinks they are doing a bad job at anything? Maybe that is just an American attitude. This was a German company.

This was a large utility company. They had decided that e-learning was important to their future, so they did what most big companies do, they told one of their HR guys to investigate and gave him a budget. He attended conferences, he heard sales pitches, he hired people, and soon enough he was building some e-learning programs.

After a while he began to feel that he had been had. He needed a learning management system. He needed the services of a variety of companies who wanted to build e-learning for him. He acquired various tools, books, consultants, and employees, but in the end he felt that what he was being sold wasn't very good and therefore what he himself was building wasn't very good. He invited me to see what he and his team had built.

I warned him that I was going to hate it, as I warn everyone whose software I am about to review. I always hate the software I see. "Why," you wonder, "haven't you ever seen anything you liked?" Well, in a word . . . "No."

Of course I am a harsh judge, but the reason that I am always unhappy with what I see is more complex than that. No matter how many of them I see . . .

Today's e-Learning or Educational Software Programs Always Seem to Contain Major Design Flaws

Flaw #1. Telling, Not Doing

One flaw I see every time is that telling tends to dominate the experience. Everyone seems to know that people learn by doing, but somehow e-learning designers can't seem to remember it. Maybe it's because people keep telling it to them. Every e-learning program seems to want to tell you the company policy or have the president of the company welcome you to the system, or tell you the right thing to do and then ask you to do it, or ask you a question and then tell you the right answer. Or, as was the case with my German client, they gave a lot of their budget over to a graphic arts company that created the coolest little animated character who showed you around an otherwise mind-numbing system.

Flaw #2. Cleverness, Not Fun

e-Learning designers know that e-learning should be fun, but the material they are teaching is usually not a laugh riot. So they introduce a cartoon character, spend lots of money on first-class animation, and have the character introduce topics in what is supposed to be a fun and satisfying way. And while these characters are quite often rather appealing, their educational value hardly justifies the money spent on them. In a sense the software is just a come-on: It seems appealing, it looks like it is going to be fun, but all the animation and humor is intended to hide the dull experience you are about to have with actual material to be learned.

Flaw #3. No Stories

A third common flaw is the lack of good storytelling. This one is odd because it is so easy to avoid. The first "telling, not doing" flaw is actually hard to figure out how to get around. The "animated character" flaw is a more subtle trap because on the surface there seems to be nothing wrong with incorporating humor and clever graphics into your learning software. The "storyless" flaw is harder to understand. How hard is it to collect a few good stories from the company's collective experience and put them in the software? No matter how boring the software, at least people would remember a well-told story, especially if it were told by someone they knew or it related to some experience they had had. But invariably the e-learning designers, desperate to put learning objects into their learning management system, have left out the stories, which was all anyone was going to remember anyway.

Flaw #4. Relentless Quizzes

The fourth flaw is the most common. e-Learning designers love quizzes it seems. Every other screen seems to be a test of some sort, asking you what you want to do or asking you what you think the right answer is to some issue you don't care about or based on something you supposedly just read or in something you are about to do. School is all tests these days, so I guess e-learning designers think that is because educational theorists think quizzes are the essence of good instructional design, when the real reason has to do with every politician's current obsession with measurable outcomes.

MEANWHILE, BACK IN GERMANY,
THEY WANT HELP . . .

To make a long story short, this German utility company showed me software that had a cute animated character telling you things you didn't want to know and asking you questions you didn't care about the answer to, about a system you didn't want to learn how to use all that much in the first place, and weren't going to learn to use by being told about it . . . all with nary a story to be found.

The only unusual part of this story is that the man who was in charge of it all didn't much like his programs either. He wanted help.

HOW DID THE GERMAN HR GUY KNOW THAT HE NEEDED HELP? *His customers (the people in the courses he built) were complaining, but that's not as bad as it might sound. Quite often, such complaints are explained away by stating that the customers were not ready for e-learning or saying that they would have to get used to it because the company decided it was more economical to do it this way. This is the point where some compromise is usually made and everyone agrees that a "blended approach" would be best—which means as far as I can tell that they won't get rid of all their classes and thus will save a few training jobs.*

  I think he knew that things were bad because he had read my book (Designing World Class e-Learning) *and realized that he had made every mistake I outlined. Although I might note that plenty of others have read this book under similar circumstances and not drawn the same conclusion.*

So I arrived in Germany with the task of teaching his team . . .

HOW TO DO E-LEARNING RIGHT IN THREE DAYS

I started by talking to them about learning, which I did because they expected it. (As you may know by now, I really don't think that telling people about learning will cause them to change their behaviors one iota.) I showed them some educational software that I think is good and we discussed what might be improved and how it compared to what they had built. And while discussions like this are good, still I knew that this wasn't going to help them learn how to do it any better either.

  What next?

Start with a Few Rules of Thumb

My favorite rules of thumb for building e-learning are to *ask experts about what goes wrong in their companies* and to *start people thinking about training as a kind of just-in-time remediation*, instead of school that prepares you for events that will take place years later after you have long forgotten the preparation.

RULES OF THUMB FOR BUILDING E-LEARNING

- Ask experts about what goes wrong in their companies.
- Start people thinking about training as a kind of just-in-time remediation.
- See e-learning as being about doing.

But mostly I try to get them to *see e-learning as being about doing*. It is about doing in two ways, of course. One issue is what employees will learn to do better. Another is what designers must learn to do differently. The best way to approach both of these at the same time is to create a simulated design exercise. *Instead of talking about what they were doing wrong, I suggested that we simply start to do something right.*

I asked them what their next e-learning project was going to be and they said new hire training, so I suggested we start the process together the next morning. I asked them to bring the expert on new hires to the table.

Bring on the SME

The team I was training sat across from the expert, and I sat to the side. I said that I would comment on what they were doing as I saw fit.

The fact is they had no idea what to do at this point. They had never started a project in this way. I mentioned that getting stories from the expert was an important first step to building any training program and understanding what needed to be taught was another and that the two were quite related. I suggested they start.

They sat there frozen.

I said, "Well, ask him a question."

"We don't know what to ask" was the somewhat testy response.

"Well, what would you need to find out before you start?" I said.

There was a brief discussion, and finally one of the more aggressive members of the team asked: "What does a new hire need to know?"

> HADN'T THEY BEEN LISTENING? *I almost fell over. Here I had been talking about learning by doing for a full day and it really hadn't penetrated. I had talked about the difference between recognition memory and recall memory. I had talked about the difference between conscious knowledge and implicit knowledge. I had talked about "knowing how" versus "knowing that."*
>
> *None of this had penetrated.*
>
> *Why I found this surprising I don't know. I always say that you can't learn by listening. Somehow I supposed that didn't include listening to me.*

The expert responded that there was a new hire manual and that everything that a new hire needed to know was contained in it. Next question.

I loved that guy. What a great answer. He also knew that it was a stupid question.

I asked the team what was wrong with the question they had asked. They responded defensively, saying that they needed to know what new hires needed to know and so they asked and what was wrong with that?

I said: "Well, it is an awful question. Can you figure out why?"

They had figured out that it was bad question from the expert's response, but they really didn't know how to improve on it.

I suggested they . . .

Try Thinking About Doing Rather Than Knowing

They asked, "What should a new hire know how to do?"
The expert responded with an absurdly long list of things, all of which were in the new hire manual as well.

I asked if they could figure out what to do.

They could not.

We sat there in silence.

Finally I said: "What is the biggest mistake that new hires make when they are first on the job?"

The expert's face lit up. He began to tell a story about some complex software that kept breaking and how new hires were clueless about how this software worked and so they couldn't answer customers' questions when they called in to complain about the software.

Huh?

I thought this was a new hire program. Rules, benefits, how we hate sexual harassment, that sort of thing.

"Nah," he said (or whatever the German equivalent was).

"What is it that these new hires are doing?" I asked.

"They answer the phone," he told me.

"Really? What about?"

"We sell software to other utility companies. It is complex and doesn't always work. Companies call up and ask difficult questions. The new hires can't know the answers right away, so they don't do so well for a long while, until they get the complex software issues down."

"So you don't want a new hire training program at all," I said.

"We don't?"

"No, you need a program to train people to answer the phone and do customer service. We have done plenty of those kinds of programs. They have nothing in common with new hire training."

And there you have it. *The reason why most training is so bad.* Unbelievably often, the people who write the training do what they were asked to do. They build what they were asked to build. But the people who are doing the asking don't always know what they want.

The reason why most training is so bad. The people who write the training do what they were asked to do. They build what they were asked to build.

WHAT TO DO INSTEAD

Think about what the company really needs, not what they ask for.

Moreover, the designers of the training don't know how to ask the right questions to find out what the company really needs. *Learning to interview experts is the cornerstone of the process of the design of training.* Teaching your designers to interview is more important than teaching them to build software.

What Are the Right Questions to Find Out What Is Really Needed?

1. What are employees having trouble doing properly?

I am not sure that the others matter all that much given the overall significance of number 1. But here are some more:

2. Can you tell me a story of when an employee didn't know what to do and it caused a big problem for the company?

3. Under what circumstance do employees do the wrong thing, even though they have been told how to do the right thing?

4. What problems are causing the company real trouble right now?

5. What are the key things an employee needs to know how to do in this company?

These five questions have worked well for us over the years. They are reasonable things to ask experts, and they usually produce responses you can work with. The questions about problems are especially important for designing training. Every time you find a problem you have an opportunity for training.

Well, almost every time . . .

Some Things Simply Can't Be Taught

At Wal-Mart they had all kinds of fun problems to tell us about when we asked our questions. My favorite involved a cashier interrupted by the phone while she was checking a customer out. She kept talking on the phone and the customer started getting angry. This didn't stop the phone conversation, however. The cashier just kept on talking. So the customer's complaints just kept growing louder. The cashier's solution was to hit the customer over the head with the phone. A novel method of customer relations to be sure.

So now that we know this error, what do we do about it? Do we create a module where you are told never to hit the customer, no matter how angry you are? Or do we discuss how destruction of company property is a bad thing? Do we design a course in anger management? Do we simply ignore this incident as a one-time oddity?

It may very well not be an oddity, but we do have to ignore it. We cannot train people to avoid playing the fool. Some folks are simply foolish.

So the questions were good ones to ask, and the answer was great fun to hear, but it didn't result in a teaching point. Some things simply can't be taught.

◊   ◊   ◊

Jump Start Your Training

Some do's and don'ts:

- Don't tell anybody anything in an e-learning program.
- Don't use graphics just because they are cute.
- Don't hide boring material in a pretty costume.
- Don't forget that the software itself must tell a story.
- Don't use e-learning as an excuse to create a multiple-choice test.
- Don't confuse yourself with the idea that "blended learning" is any more than a political compromise.

- Do remember to ask experts about what isn't working in the company.
- Do ask what employees need to learn to do better at their jobs.
- Do ask what instructional designers are doing wrong.
- Do think of e-learning as "just-in-time remediation."
- Do ask experts for their "horror stories."
- Do not imagine that all horror stories teach an important lesson.
- Don't ask what an employee needs to know.
- Do ask about what employees will be expected to be able to do.
- Don't confuse employee status with employee function— doing errors transcend status.
- Don't think that those who have requested training know what they actually need.
- Do start questioning experts about problems in the company's business.
- Do learn to interview experts properly.
- Do focus training designs on teaching points.

5

Enron Fixes Their Communication Problems

THOUGHTS ON WHEN TO JUST SAY NO—
LIKE WHEN YOUR COMPANY ASKS FOR A TRAINING COURSE

This sounds like an odd subject. And one to which I wouldn't have given a moment's thought if my company hadn't built an e-learning program for helping Enron employees communicate.

Many people who have written about Enron have commented how communication seems to have been a major issue in its demise:

> "Such a community requires collaboration and communication throughout the organization. Too many corporate managers are well trained in 'hard,' quantifiable, technical skills, but very poorly trained in 'soft' skills, such as empa-

thy, communication, validation, conflict management, and community building."

(Lessons from the Enron Debacle: Corporate Culture Matters!, Paul T.P. Wong, www.meaning.ca/articles/ lessons_from_enron.htm)

"*Finally, we can't ignore Enron's communication snafus. By now, all readers know what's happened to Enron, one of the country's largest companies, now bankrupt. We maintain that their failure can be attributed to total contempt for communication.*"

(2001 "BIMBO OF THE YEAR" AWARDED, www.spaethcom.com/bimbo_december2001.html)

"*Some ways that corporate leaders and communications gurus are adapting to the new post-Enron climate: Corporate communications experts are urging more frequent communications with employees, from face-to-face meetings to Webcasts and satellite broadcasts. GE has added a new level of access and communication to regular meetings between CEO Immelt and analysts: they are now broadcast on GE's Website. According to Immelt, 'We want to be touched and felt and viewed and discovered. I think that plays to our strengths.'*"

(AFTER ENRON: More Employee Communication, More Visible Leaders, www.jackmorton.com/360/ industry_news/mar02_in2.asp)

As it happened, Enron knew it had a communication problem. And, get this: they thought we (by this I mean the e-learning company I had founded) could solve it! They asked us to build an e-learning program to fix their communication problems.

Enron asked my company to build an interactive web-based program to improve the communication skills of its employees at all management levels. The program was supposed to "give managers practical experience in communication," and also "show them how strong communication skills could help them achieve their business goals." One wonders who was issuing these orders from on high in Enron. The people we were dealing with presumably were not the ones who failed to communicate with the public about the underhanded dealings at Enron.

Enron, it turns out, had an ethics booklet that outlines Enron's core values. One of these is Communication:

> *"Communication: We believe that information is meant to move and that information moves people."*

Whatever that means. They didn't even seem to be capable of communication when they wrote about communication. The issue here, for me anyway, is the use of the term "communication."

And why is this a training problem, you ask? Because saying you need to teach employees to communicate better is a nice way of missing the real problems in a company.

Did Enron Have a Communication Problem?

To better answer this question let's consider what Enron actually thought that their communication problem was.

Their motivation in contacting us had to do with a survey of their employees that they had conducted:

- 59 percent of employees said decisions were not communicated well.
- 54 percent said they did not feel free to voice their opinions openly.

- 55 percent said the company didn't act effectively on employee suggestions.
- 70 percent said communication was not good across departmental lines.
- 61 percent said they were not encouraged to challenge established procedures and policies.

Enron asked us to build computer simulations that would train employees in situations meant to emulate the five trouble spots in the survey. The people in my company interviewed 132 Enron employees in order to find real-life experiences and stories about communication breakdowns within the organization. From this information they developed computer simulations using the *goal-based scenario* approach I have been using for years.

> *Saying you need to teach employees to communicate better is a nice way of missing the real problems in a company.*

HOW GOAL-BASED SCENARIOS WORK   *In each scenario, the user is presented with an overview of the situation and then has the opportunity to do some background research by poring over scenario-specific resources. These resources include things like an employee's last performance review or notes about an idea an employee has come up with. The scenarios are much harder for people who haven't prepared themselves properly.*

The people who were interviewed identified two common types of mistakes Enron managers made in their communication:

1. People don't use the right medium for communication (e.g., too many e-mails).

2. People don't always effectively get across what they're trying to say when they do talk face-to-face with employees.

This is pretty funny stuff actually. Enron employees believed that communications were shaky at Enron because too many e-mails were being sent and because people couldn't figure out how to say what they mean. Maybe so. Maybe so.

Because of these results, each scenario we built featured two different kinds of decisions. The first involved making a choice about what medium to communicate in (e.g., phone, e-mail, or in person). The user is asked to defend his or her reasons for picking that course of action and receives tutoring on both incorrect choices and faulty justifications.

The second type of decision consisted of interactions with fictional peers, with the focus on how to communicate strategic decisions (e.g., what to say). If the user failed to make the correct choice, he or she received advice and tutoring, complete with links to a small performance support system full of tips, expert stories, and resources for effective communication.

FOR EXAMPLE

In "A Matter of Meetings," the user plays the role of a new lead on a project requiring collaboration from several different departments. The user's goal is to get the project team back on track by addressing its communication problems. The scenario begins when a team member complains to the user about how the old project lead ran meetings. She gives an example of a failed and unfocused meeting.

When the user has done enough research, he or she can prepare for the meeting by sending out an e-mail, deciding (1) Whom to invite to the meeting, (2) What to focus the meeting on, (3) The goals of the meeting, and (4) Action items. For each, the user must select the response(s) he or she feels are most appropriate; the system provides brief tutoring for incorrect or omitted choices.

After the user sends the e-mail, the simulation jumps ahead to the meeting. Here the user must do and say the right things to move the meeting forward and effectively address the team's communication problems. When the user mouses over a strategy choice, "What this might sound like" text appears in a box below, giving the user an idea of how each potential choice could be articulated.

Each choice leads to a video response from the team members at the meeting. If the user chooses to "Discuss past communication problems with participants" at the outset of the meeting, for example, an argument breaks out among the team members. For incorrect responses, "What went wrong?" tutoring details the action the user chose, why the team reacted the way it did, and what a better approach might be. After the user gets through the meeting, he or she must then decide what strategic actions to take regarding team members who missed the meeting. For each step, the user must choose an action and justify it.

When the user successfully completes the scenario, he or she goes to a reflection page that details where the user made mistakes in several key skill areas, including preparing for the meeting, focusing on meeting objectives, soliciting feedback, and following up on decisions.

We have been building goal-based scenarios like these on computers for many years. They are great ways to get someone to experience a situation without actually being there. For example, we built one for the U.S. Environmental Protection Agency to teach EPA officials how to handle a public meeting.

In the simulation they ran fictional meetings full of oddball characters with whom they had to interact. Each character did and said what people typically do and say in EPA meetings, and mistaken responses were dealt with by having to now deal with even angrier characters. EPA officials interrupted to give advice on what to do.

> *Goal-based scenarios help people practice skills that are difficult to practice in real life without causing them (and their organization) great difficulties.*

It is obvious that the people in my company were trying to utilize the same ideas for an Enron meeting.

What Went Wrong?

The real issue is what the problem was in the first place. The EPA knew what its problem was: new employees got clobbered in public meetings. Did Enron know what its problems were? Was their communication problem a matter of meetings?

Here are excerpts of an article I found at EffectiveIntranets.Com (http://effectiveintranets.com/cgibin/wwwthreads/showthreaded.pl?Board=news&Number=102):

Jerry Stevenson

Enron's Top Notch Electronic Comms—4/01/2002
Shooting the (electronic) messenger
The fanciest communication tools are only as good as the people using them.

   Last fall, Enron CEO Kenneth Lay held a company-wide meeting to allay concerns that the company was in serious trouble. And what better way to assemble his far-flung troops for a chat than through the company intranet?

"The third quarter is looking great," Lay told an Enron employee during the Sept. 26 "E-speak," three weeks before the company announced $638 million in third-quarter losses.

Asked by another employee what would happen when Enron's accounting practices "come home to roost" in the next ten years, Lay said, "I would guess ten years from now our net income will be four- to six-fold what it is today, and our market cap will be eight to ten times what it is today."

He went on to urge employees to invest further in Enron, telling them the stock price was "an incredible bargain" at the then-current price of about $25.

A short time after that meeting, Enron publicly admitted it had kept hundreds of millions of dollars in debt off the company books and misled its employees—through the company intranet and other communication vehicles—into thinking it was a sound business. Enron stock became worthless, and many employees lost their jobs and their pensions.

But the Enron debacle also raises questions for business leaders—and communicators—all over America. Can executives regain the implicit trust of employees? Will communicators—and electronic-communication vehicles—ever be looked at the same again? Will companies abandon their use of the intranet and online executive chats for fear that whatever is stated in those internal vehicles could bite them on the, well, bottom line?

This much is clear: Your company's communications tools are only as good as the people using them. Enron had a weekly online newspaper; upward communication programs where employees could pose questions to the executives and receive a response within three days; and "E-Think," a think tank that encouraged employees to come up with and bounce ideas off one another online.

And there's the infamous "E-Speak," where every other week Ken Lay or an Enron board member would participate in an e-mail forum. Employees worldwide would ask questions that would be answered on the spot.

Enron also used sophisticated plasma screens inside elevators and an in-house production team that created "30-second spots" to keep employees informed about company news.

But all of this communication goes for naught if a company uses those tools to deliver false messages.

Let's look at the list of Enron's communication problems again:

- 59 percent of employees said decisions were not communicated well.

- 54 percent said they did not feel free to voice their opinions openly.

- 55 percent said the company didn't act effectively on employee suggestions.

- 70 percent said communication was not good across departmental lines.

- 61 percent said they were not encouraged to challenge established procedures and policies.

What is wrong with these results? Consider the third one on the list. I used the software my company had written to see what they did about this one. I played the role of a manager and someone came to see me to make a suggestion about how things could be improved. One of my choices was to tell him to make an appointment for some time next week. I chose that and was instructed that I should have met with him immediately.

Think about that for a minute. Quite the communications remedy.

Another problem that Enron identified—this one not in the top five—was that its employees didn't feel that their suggestions were being paid attention to. Is this a communication problem?

I don't know about you, but if I felt my company was unreceptive to suggestions I wouldn't concentrate on speed as a means of improving that receptivity. Unless, of course, I wasn't trying to do any more than make it appear that the company was receptive to suggestions, knowing full well that there was plenty of stuff to hide and it wasn't all that much fun to hear that someone had found an irregularity of some sort.

One thing is clear. Defining inattention and ineffective action as a communication problem lets a lot of people off the hook. The solution to making employees feel that you are open to suggestions, was, according to Enron, listening to what they had to suggest right away.

> ANOTHER EXAMPLE   *61 percent said they were not encouraged to challenge established procedures and policies. Really? Quel suprise! Now, in retrospect, this seems to be an indictment of Enron, but really, how many companies want their procedures and policies challenged?*

OUR e-LEARNING SOLUTION?

You guessed it. Managers role play listening to policy suggestions and are coached to say, "That was a great idea and it will certainly get discussed." This for a fictional (and thus presumably non-great) idea. So now all ideas are great. What a solution to being receptive to new ideas. Our communication module was actually an obfuscation model. It taught employees how to fake listening.

> *Of course, you are thinking: then why were you part of building this stuff? Well, actually, I wasn't. It was done during a period of time where I was not involved in the training part of our business. But even so, I included a description of the Enron module in my book* Designing World Class e-Learning, *so I must have thought it was okay. I just thought what we were doing at my company was better than the junk other companies were putting out, which was really the point of the book. That's not a particularly good answer I know, but while I was writing that book I began to see that there were some serious problems in everyone's approach to training, which is, in part, why I am writing this one.*

I had wearied of much of what I was asked to work on in the training business precisely because of this kind of problem. What kind of problem is that, you ask?

The real problem was . . .

Thinking All Problems Are Training Problems

Trainers have the idea that all problems are really training problems. I must confess that as an educational reformer I have a lot of sympathy with that point of view. Whenever I see an ill in society I always think that it could have been remedied with just a little more education or a little better education for the people involved. You don't grow up to do dumb things if you have been taught how to do reasonable things.

> *Trainers have the idea that all problems are really training problems.*

But when dealing with fully formed adults, while you can teach new skills easily enough, remediating old habits is a different story altogether. Enron employees felt just a bit frightened to express themselves, did they? That's what I get out of the survey results. Well then, how about getting rid of the culture of fear? How do we do that? Certainly not by labeling the problem a communication problem. In fact, it is obvious, hindsight being twenty-twenty, that there was a reason that a culture of fear was prevalent. There was something to hide. When people are afraid of being found out for the dark thing they are engaged in, they tend be less than open. That culture permeates all the way down so that people at Enron who were hiding nothing were probably fearful just because that's the way things were done at Enron.

> *Our communication module was actually an obfuscation model. It taught employees how to fake listening.*

THE SOLUTION TO ALL THIS?

Well, from a PR point of view, calling it a communications issue and starting communication training seems like a peachy idea. But sometimes you have to ask what the real problem is. You may not like what you see.

How do we teach communication? This sounds like a legitimate training issue, but it simply isn't. Communication skills seem like something one can teach. Simply focus on the problems in communication and provide training for each one. With that in mind let's look at what the Enron survey says, one more time:

- 59 percent of employees said decisions were not communicated well.
- 54 percent said they did not feel free to voice their opinions openly.
- 55 percent said the company didn't act effectively on employee suggestions.
- 70 percent said communication was not good across departmental lines.
- 61 percent said they were not encouraged to challenge established procedures and policies.

> *"How do we teach communication?" sounds like a legitimate training issue, but it simply isn't.*

Now let's suppose that we were not allowed to use the word *communication* to describe these problems. What words could we use? I suggest these five:

Clarity

Freedom

Listening

Silos

Fear

Which of these things can be taught in a training session (electronic or otherwise)? Would you like to attend training on how to be less fearful that your company will not react well to what you say and think?

Is this a training issue? Can we train bosses to treat their employees in such a way that they are unafraid to speak their minds? Well, no.

Why not?

Because training and real life are different things. We can teach people to say some words about how they should treat people, but the issue is the reward system after all. If the company rewards people who are tough on their employees (or run a tight ship, to put a positive spin on it), then it cannot simultaneously reward people for being touchy feely with their employees. In fact this is a hiring issue not a training issue. A company that hires tough guys isn't one that hires nice guys. We are talking about different cultures here. Now I never met anyone at Enron, so I have no personal take on what kind of people they hired. But I can guess, given the employee survey and the ensuing debacle at Enron, that openness wasn't rewarded because openness wasn't valued.

> *All too often training people (me included) allow themselves to get sucked into the baloney that a company is selling.*

All too often training people (me included) allow themselves to get sucked into the baloney that a company is selling. "We have a communication problem" turned out to be code for: *We realize that this is an uptight and secretive place, but it is like that because we are doing some pretty underhanded things, so it would be nice if you could just make it seem like we really care about these issues by teaching people to behave in a way that they could not possibly learn to behave from training. Be assured we will do everything we can to undermine the training you provide by failing to change the workplace one bit.*

The problem is twofold. First, there are some things you simply cannot learn in training. Second, when training is really a ruse to hide a deeper problem, it won't work (even if that kind of training could work in principle if it wasn't done as a ruse).

So Can You Teach Communication?

Is communication a subject that is in principle unteachable in training? At first glance the answer to the "unteachableness" question would seem to be "no." After all one can get a degree in communications—it is a legitimate field of inquiry in many universities, and it comprises a set of skills we all want to improve upon. So the answer must be "yes."

> *There are some things you simply cannot learn in training. Plus, when training is really a ruse to hide a deeper problem, it won't work (even if that kind of training could work in principle if it wasn't done as a ruse).*

For years I have been preaching that the big three issues in education are reasoning, communication, and human relations. I have said many times that schools must strive to enable students to learn these skills, that they are more important in daily life by far than physics, mathematics, or ancient history. So obviously, I think communication can be taught, right?

Well, no.

Communication Skills Can Be Learned, But That Is a Different Statement

When I have talked about how those subjects constitute the big three in education, I also pointed out that none of them can be taught directly. Imagine a course in reasoning for example. You can easily imagine that a school's course in reasoning would come down to learning the six principles of reasoning, or diagramming the reasoning extant in a piece of text, or identifying the types of reasoning that were being employed in an argument. When school teaches a subject, it usually boils it down into something analytical (and irrelevant) that people need to learn, avoiding the skill itself altogether.

The communication schools that teach communication teach the theory of communication, or how to deal with communicative disorders, or perhaps they include a journalism program as some sort of practical implementation of communication theory. The actual skills we need for communication we learn as a result of having a goal and seeing its realization (or lack thereof) by our communicative methods. We speak, we write, we communicate, about something, with some end in mind other than the communication itself. We don't try to communicate, we try to be understood or agreed with, or we try to convince somebody of something or get someone to do something we want done.

> *The actual skills we need for communication we learn as a result of having a goal and seeing its realization (or lack thereof) by our communicative methods.*

Communication skills are learned only by practice. We practice communication with every sentence we utter. We know how well those sentences have worked when our listener says "huh?" or "really?" or "I am so happy you said that" or something in between. The outside world reinforces, for better or worse, our communication skills on a daily (or even minute-by-minute) basis. So we really don't need courses in communication; we need opportunities for communication.

Well, no, I don't really believe that either. Communication that is observed by someone else whom we trust who can comment on how well we expressed ourselves or whether we seemed to be listening or whether what we said was what we meant, can be quite valuable. In other words we can all use some tutoring with respect to the communicative efforts we engage in. (Perhaps someone could help me make this paragraph better, for example.)

But did my company do that in its Enron course? No. What it did was give people some right and wrong answers to select from that would demonstrate that they were being sympathetic to the speaker. Now I ask you, who is going to say in a simulated scenario in a course on being open to employees, that they are "too busy for a meeting right now and could you come back in a week?" No one is too busy in a simulation. People are too busy in real life, which is exactly what a simulation isn't.

The question that might be on your mind at this point is . . .

How to Tell the Difference Between Stuff That Can Be Taught and Stuff That Can't

. . . so that you know when to tell those on high who have ordered training to be built that maybe they should work on some other subject area that the company needs taught that might actually work.

Here is my rule of thumb. Take the subject to be taught and ask the following questions:

1. Are there skills that comprise this subject?
2. Can you name them?

3. Can you practice them?

4. Would you be able to tell if someone was doing them right?

5. Are mistakes honestly made and recoverable?

For Example

To take an obvious case, let's consider training to be a fire-fighter.

1. *Are there skills?* You have to do things like hold the hose, break windows, crawl under fire, and all kinds of other good stuff.

2. *Can you name them?* I can't, but firefighters can.

3. *Can you practice them?* It takes much training on real burning houses used for practice.

4. *Would you be able to tell if someone were doing them right?* Putting the fire out without getting hurt is a clear and good result.

5. *Are mistakes honestly made and recoverable?* I would assume so. One imagines that some of the best fire-fighters made some serious mistakes at first but got better over time.

So there you have it. A real subject for training. Training firefighters is definitely a good idea. Any other plan seems insane.

Another Example

Now let's look at one that isn't really a subject for training.

I will choose "thinking out of the box," a subject that comes up a great deal in conversations about what companies need to do. So let's imagine you have been asked to teach a "thinking out of the box" course by your company. Answer my five questions first:

1. *Are there skills?* I have no idea what the skills are in "out of the box thinking." I can identify the product of creative thinking when I see it, but I don't know what produces that product. (Well, I have some idea actually. I once wrote a book on creativity, but my view was that it was an attitude rather than a set of skills.)

2. *Can you name them?* No, we can't name the skills.

3. *Can you practice being creative?* You can try, but I doubt that that is what creative people do in order to become creative. They may, as children, continually be creative and then get better at it, but they are not trying to be creative—they are trying to do things that happen to be considered creative by others, which is a different thing altogether.

4. *Can you tell when someone is being creative?* Sort of. But a lot depends on context and what has come before and whether the person involved heard about those new ideas from someone else.

5. *Can you fix someone's creativity mistakes?* I am not sure what this would mean exactly, so I guess not.

This is simple, no? Some subjects are good candidates for the training department and some are not.

Then what about communication? Can it be taught? I don't think so.

The good news is that communication can be seen as a set of skills (like writing, public speaking, listening, and so on) and each of these can be taught. But you will notice Enron did not ask for a writing course (in fact we had one available—described in that same book—that I would have been proud to recommend).

So what was the problem at Enron? They got the skills wrong because they tried to design them based on a survey of problem areas which, in case you forgot, were

Clarity

Freedom

Listening

Silos

Fear

Try my five questions on those areas. Only "listening" seems like an actual skill, but I was just writing a kind of shorthand there. Really the survey said "listening and acting on what you heard" was the problem. In other words, no one did anything when employees at Enron complained. And no training course was ever going to fix that. Nor was training going to make people less fearful in an environment that had plenty to hide.

Bottom line: Be careful when your bosses ask you to build training. Sometimes you should just say "no."

◊   ◊   ◊

Jump Start Your Training

Here's a checklist for knowing the difference between things that can be taught and things that cannot.

CAN'T BE TAUGHT	CAN BE TAUGHT
Aptitudes	People Skills
Attitudes	Particular Skills
Wisdom	Decision Making
Good Judgment	Cases of Bad Judgment
Experience	Simulated Cases
Openness	Handling Customer Problems
Friendliness	Courtesy
Physical Principles	Physical Skills (by Practice)

6

Sex and Chicken

THE ROLE OF NONCONSCIOUS LEARNING—
AND HOW TO HELP ADULTS DO IT

Occasionally, I am asked by large corporations to look into their training issues. These assignments can be great fun or downright boring. Companies tend to have similar problems in training, so often I find myself saying the same thing that I said in my last engagement. It is not often that I find myself saying the same thing to a training company and to a friend, however, but this happened in the course of a very odd week recently.

The experience was odd because neither the company nor the friend was what you would call "normal." The company grosses a billion dollars a year from the fast food business. My friend doesn't gross quite that much. I don't know what he earns after all, but believe me, his numbers aren't that far off.

So they are both doing very well, thank you very much. Where they differ is in, shall we say, moral rectitude. The company seems to employ only people who wear white shirts and ties and pray a lot. Family values are mentioned quite frequently. Somehow selling chicken is seen as doing God's work.

My friend, on the other hand, lives the kind of life that many men fantasize about, and, shall we say, moral rectitude doesn't come up much. Neither does family, since my friend has never been married, but it came up when I saw him because he has decided, now that he had passed fifty, to have a child. He has no intention of getting married, however.

What does any of this have to do with training?

At first glance not much.

The meeting at the fast food company was, as I said, quite typical. Companies often believe that their training is just fine thank you, and when I have been called in they are often not quite sure why (even though they are the ones who called.) They know I build cool simulations and other training stuff, and they want to see it, is of course one reason, I suppose. They often do lots of stand up in class training and they sometimes view this like cigarette smoking, a bad habit that feels so good. So they are willing to let me explain why they shouldn't smoke, but they usually keep on smoking—too many vested interests. They have built all those classrooms and all that infrastructure after all. But deeper and often hidden are the real reasons they have called me.

"What doesn't work in the training you do now?" I ask.

"Nothing. It all works fine," they respond. They built that training after all. It must be great.

"Well then," I say, "let me ask you a different question: What goes wrong in your restaurants?"

This question usually works. Unfortunately, since I have consulted with restaurant chains before, I already know the type of answer I'll hear. "Politeness," they say. Or courtesy or rudeness, or how to deal with difficult customers or how to handle difficult situations in the restaurant. These are always the answers.

So What's the Training Department to Do?

I have an answer on how to deal with this of course, but before I talk about that answer I want to go back to my friend.

My friend had decided to have a child but he had no intention of getting married or living with his "family." He was scheming on how best to do this and was asking me all kinds of questions since I know a lot about child development and, of course, about education. I asked him, "Why only one?" He has a great many women in his life and more money than he could ever spend, so why not more? He got his arms around this idea and the questions started flying.

- Who will decide what school the kid goes to?
- Who is in charge of health decisions?
- Where should the mother and child live?

What school the kid goes to wasn't a real issue, I told him. Parents tend not to fight about such things unless there are religious issues involved. I suggested he make sure there weren't. Similarly, unless one of the women was a Christian Scientist, I doubted health decisions would be a real problem. He has four houses. I suggested that the women and children could live in any or all of them and he could visit as he wanted, the way he does now.

"Could the women have men in their lives?" he asked. At first this took me by surprise, but I guess he figured he'd lose interest, as he always had done before (which is, I suppose why he wasn't getting married and why we were having all this discussion in the first place).

"No," I said immediately, and he asked why.

> *The problem when you are trying to invent the rules of life for yourself instead of simply copying what others have done is that you can assume that people throughout history have tried many different ways to live and that the ones we have had handed down to us may well be the best.* When you invent your own rules, you are forced to examine first principles again and again, asking questions that most people never have to ask.

Such a reasonable question with such a complex answer. I decided to tell him about my daughter, Hana, when she was about one and a half. We were living in Switzerland at the time. Hana was my parents' first grandchild and they were in New York, so there were frequent phone calls back and forth and more than the occasional visit. Once during this period I got curious as to whether Hana knew the names of her grandparents. I figured she might not know the word "name" so I asked her "What does Gammy (her name for my mother) call Poppy (my father)? She immediately responded "Maaacc!!" imitating the intonation and exasperation of my mother trying to get my father's attention. I asked what my father called my mother and she said "Marge!" in a tone of an authoritative military call.

One more example: One day I noticed Hana walking in furious circles while she was talking on the phone to my parents, at one point almost bringing the phone down on her head. Now who had been teaching her that? Well . . . me. That's what I do when I talk on the phone. And it is still what my daughter does, thirty years later.

I told my friend these stories because the moral is pretty clear. *Children don't know what the critical things to attend to are in the information they receive, so they attend to all of it.* Hana was a kind of tape recorder: She attended to everything and copied as much as she could. Like a duck following the first thing that moves after it is born, thus imprinting a football as its mother if it happens to roll by, a child attends to what is around her.

Now if there is another man in the life of my friend's child, who is to tell the child that what that man does isn't worth copying just because he is not paying the bills and is not genetically related? No child cares about anything at that age besides figuring out how the world works. Whoever is in the child's world teaches that child how to behave, whether you like it or not. I figured my friend might not like the new male teacher that mommy brought home.

Another man in the house brings someone new to copy. He might be someone real good to copy, who knows? But he won't be my friend. Little by little, my friend's children would be his only genetically if he wasn't careful.

Now what does this have to do with training in the fast food company that called me in for a consult?

Everything.

People are pretty well formed by the time they are only half-way through their childhood. All their little habits, attitudes, and general ways of being are formed real early on.

So How Do You Get Employees Not to Be Rude to Customers or Learn How to Handle Difficulties with Aplomb?

You teach them when they are four or five years old. Those behaviors are imprinted early on by watching mom or dad—or whoever is on the scene most of the time. The problem is that some businesses, like fast food restaurants, are not necessarily getting the cream of society for $6 an hour. These workers didn't necessarily have great role models who taught them how to cope when the going gets tough.

So there are only two answers to this problem.

Answer #1. Hire the Right People

This is the first, and best, answer. Check up on their families. Make sure they treat those they know with civility and they may well do so at the restaurant as well.

While this may seem like obvious advice, it is rarely followed. The company I was consulting for does do this. They spend a great deal of time in the hiring process and try very hard to get the right sort of folks. What goes wrong there then?

That is easy to guess at. Unless you put someone in a situation, you never really know how he or she will respond. You can ask anything you like, and he can learn to say what you want to hear, but imprinting is a nonconscious process. *It is the nonconscious processes that matter most.*

> *What is a nonconscious process? James Galwey describes this best in the* Inner Game of Tennis. *He says that when you are trying to remember to keep your elbow straight because you were told that would help you hit the ball right, you find yourself telling yourself or reminding yourself to do that. "Who is talking to whom exactly?" Galwey asks.*
>
> *The idea that there is an inner self who is in charge who can be reasoned with is ubiquitous in our everyday behavior. But does this make sense? If we can tell our inner self what to do, what is preventing our inner selves from listening? The answer is that you can't really talk to the nonconscious self. Hana can catch herself walking in circles while talking on the phone and she can stop the*

behavior, but when she isn't paying attention her nonconscious self starts walking.

The nonconscious self wins every time when it is left to its own devices.

And how do we educate people in nonconscious processes? How do we get the employee to change her natural instinct to throttle a customer who annoys her? This leads us to the second answer.

Answer #2. Practice

Get them to deal with crises on a regular basis and they will get better at handling them. This is best done in simulation, of course, the more realistic the better. So what does this mean in reality? It means that in order to imprint a new set of nonconscious behaviors one has to bring up the new behaviors in the same way that one would bring them up in a child. To put this another way, you can't just talk about them.

> *To imprint new nonconscious behaviors, you have to bring them up the same way you would in a child—you can't just talk about them.*

Companies love to set up lists of rules, or values, or principles, that all employees must learn to mouth. The value of this is zip, nothing, worthless. The reason is simple: you are talking to the wrong self. The inner self, the nonconscious self, the imprinting child, is simply not listening. To reach that self one has to go back to the methods that imprint behavior in the first place.

What All This Means Is . . .

Starting simply and using a reward system that is very simple. Remember that children learn behaviors by watching others. But if you think that that means that you should show video-tapes of good behavior, you are thinking wrong. Yet again, you would be talking to the wrong self. Instead, you need to strictly enforce punishment for bad behavior in front of future actors. Let me explain.

It may seem that people skills are easy and other skills are difficult, so it is tempting to hire a hostess or a cashier who has had little training. In fact, these skills are the hardest. In a restaurant, where those skills are most valued, one should have to work one's way up to such positions. In other words, have people fry French fries before they ever come into contact with a customer. Let them observe good customer contact behavior, however, while they are working at the fry station. And let them also observe bad behavior dealt with swiftly—which would eliminate it from something that could be copied because the new employee would see what happened when such behavior occurred and would nonconsciously be averse to trying to behave that way. Actions speak louder than words, as we know.

> *Bad behavior dealt with swiftly eliminates it as something that can be copied.*

This is not all that can be done, of course. The value of the computer in training is to replicate realistic situations that can be played out without risk of failure. The air flight simulator is a much better way to learn how to fly a plane than just taking off in one. Crashes don't hurt in simulation.

So should restaurants build and use restaurant simulators? It is really hard to believe that they don't. Practice, practice, practice. *If you want people to exhibit certain behaviors, they need a chance to practice those behaviors again and again.* How costly would it be to build an elaborate simulator of a restaurant where every role in the restaurant was played out and a new employee needed to interact well in the simulation, where nightmarish circumstances tested his mettle, before going into that role in the real restaurant? It is cheaper in the long run to build such a simulator than to deal with the fallout over lost customers who complain that they are being treated rudely.

The point: we need to start the imprinting process again. People continue to learn throughout life, adopting new role models as adults and practicing new behaviors. But they rarely learn by being told. They learn by watching and by doing. If the senior people in the restaurant are really courteous both to employees and to customers, it might well rub off.

Nonconscious teaching is the deepest. The duck didn't decide to follow the football and my daughter didn't decide to walk in circles.

◊　◊　◊

Jump Start Your Thinking

SOME DO'S AND DON'TS

- Do wonder what is not working in your company.
- Do use mistakes made every day at your company as the bases of the training courses you decide to build.
- Do examine why the processes that are executed at your company are in place.

- Don't try to teach what should have been taught when the employee was five years old.

- Do realize that an employee's personality and attitudes are (for the most part) unchangeable.

- Don't try to tell employees not to do what they are naturally inclined to do.

- Do make employees practice proper behavior again and again.

- Do not confuse the conscious listener with the nonconscious actor.

- Do use simulations that allow employees to practice proper behavior repeatedly.

- Do use simulations instead of actual experience when teaching people skills.

- Do allow employees to imprint proper behavior by watching it in live action.

- Do teach the nonconscious self by constant contact with proper role models.

7

I Can't Remember Whether I Ate the Whole Thing

ON THE DIFFERENCE BETWEEN EVENT MEMORY AND
PROCEDURAL MEMORY—AND HOW PRACTICE HAS TO FIGURE IN

When I turned forty I threw myself a birthday party in Paris. I was spending a sabbatical year there and the French government was willing to pay for a conference about Artificial Intelligence (my field at the time). So with little convincing, some of my more food-oriented friends (and some of their wives) were happy to show up for my party. As I am not the dancing and balloons type, the only issue was to select the restaurant.

At the time, Jamin was a restaurant in Paris that was number one on everyone's "best restaurant in the world" list. It was not easy to get into, but I was able to reserve the private room for a party of fifteen for the night of my birthday.

I am a food nut, so of course I knew the food at this restaurant and thought it was terrific. The problem I had in constructing my birthday dinner menu was that there were so many dishes that I thought were terrific that I had trouble choosing between them. I kept adding one appetizer after another. The chef thought this was odd, of course, but he became visibly upset when I suggested that we simply not have a main dish and just do lots of appetizers. Chefs in France are like sports stars in the United States. No one ever tells them they are wrong or "let's not do it your way," but I did, and the chef gave in. I think he just figured Americans were crazy anyway and so it didn't really matter.

I had a problem with desserts too. Jamin made the best crème brulee I had ever had, but there was other good stuff as well. So when we finished our negotiations, this was the menu we decided on:

Ravioli de Langoustines au Chou

***

Galette de Truffes aux Oignons et Lard Fume

***

Homard Meuniere aux Epices

***

Foie Gras Chaud a la Creme de Lentilles

***

Ris de Veau Truffe aux Asperges

***

Fromage Frais et Affines

Chaud-Froid de Pommes a la Pistache

Chaud-Froid Caramelisee a la Cassonade

***

Cafe Express et Mignardises

***

Chocolats fins

Which is, in English:

shrimp ravioli

truffle and onion pie

lobster in a spicy sauce

hot goose liver in a lentil cream sauce

sweetbreads in a truffle sauce with asparagus

cheese

cold apples with a hot sauce of pistachio

caramelized cream (crème brulee)

coffee

little chocolates

I just had to have the truffle pie again and the goose liver was so great. Well you get the idea. So it was an odd meal. But each dish was extraordinary.

You are of course wondering why I am telling you about a meal I ate almost twenty years ago. Because it has to do with training.

More precisely, it has to do with . . .

How and What People Remember

Eighty years ago or so, a very famous psychologist named Bartlett ran an experiment that became world famous in the world of human memory research. He told a number of people an Eskimo folk tale. Now as you may know, folk tales from cultures with which one is not familiar can seem awfully weird. They often make references to events, myths, gods, procedures, and such that a twentieth century Englishman (Bartlett's subjects were English, as was he) could not possibly understand. A twenty-first century American would fare no better.

A Lesson from Human Memory Research

When Bartlett's subjects were asked to recall a story, their recall diminished over time, but also became more coherent.

So when the subjects were told the Eskimo folk tale, they didn't necessarily understand it all that well. Over a period of a few years, Bartlett asked his various subjects to recall the story he had originally read to them. Their recall diminished over time, but also became more coherent. In other words, the bits and pieces that made no sense were forgotten or simply made into something that did make sense to the hearer. Details were of course left out, but less obviously, new stuff was added.

People like a coherent story and have trouble remembering one that is confusing, so they conveniently forget the stuff that doesn't work for them. Hence . . .

My Human Memory Experiment

I found Bartlett's work exciting when I read it years ago. And then I had an idea. I wondered if I could conduct my own similar experiment on my friends. They had eaten this phenomenal meal. They were, for the most part, food nuts like myself. Did they remember what they had eaten? So three years later I called a few of them. Here is what they said:

ANDREW: My recollection is that there were on the order of six or seven courses. I can't remember the order in which these courses were. There was at least the following, I think. I can't remember what its technical name is—it was thyroid gland of something or other. Sweetbreads? Anyway, there was thyroid gland, there was a delicious, lightly cooked, I think it was goose liver. There was an early course—it was something with truffles on it? At least three of the courses were on the nature of what we call offal. Spelled offal. I don't know how offal is defined but generally, everything in that category includes inside organs of creatures. There were—dessert—I know why I'm having a hard time recalling what we ate, because there was a lot of food in total, but there was no course that I could identify as the central course of the meal, in the way in which more traditionally known gastronomes would consider it. There was no course that was the main course, at least not that I could recognize as the main course. It was a long time ago and I'm not doing very well at remembering it. I recall the thyroid gland, I recall the goose liver. There was this early thing with truffles but I can't remember what it was and trying to recall what the dessert was. I remember chocolate oranges, creme de caramel—I'm having a hard time recalling it.

ANATOLE: We ate ravioli with lobster, we ate this wonderful dessert which was something like a spider web. I don't remember specific dishes . . . but if I think more—I have to imagine the progressions from ravioli to the dessert. Towards-the-middle needs to be reconstructed. There was something with fish. I remember most of the fish kinds of dishes. I think there may have been some sweetbreads of some sort, but I'm not sure.

JERRY: What did we eat? Okay—we went to this two-story restaurant in Paris and we had a bizarre dinner of huge selections, in which it was all appetizers and desserts. And it was something like four appetizers and three desserts and then there were cheeses and wines and broken wine glasses. The thing that comes to mind first was the best creme brulee I ever had with some crumbled stuff on the bottom, which was vanilla. Among the appetizers—I don't remember it very well. I basically would have to fake it. There were—I don't usually have visual memories—I think maybe the presentation was more remarkable than the taste. This is interesting—I think I'm not going to do very well.

DON: What we ate. No, I can remember a large number of the activities and I can remember many courses and that there was a lot of champagne. Can I remember what we ate? No. I suppose if you gave me an appropriate setting and let me relax a bit, I could recall things. For example, as I start thinking about it now, I can remember where I was sitting and I can remember various courses, and I can remember that I. . . . What was the entree? Oh, someone refused to eat it, so I ate his, it was so very good. So I'm sure I could recall it. But no, no particular names come to mind. Not even the entree, which I now remember eating a second helping of.

ELLIOT: We had eight courses of wonderful things—the best part was that I sat next to two women who were on diets so I had three of everything, I had these raviolis in something or other and I thought that was astounding, with sweetbreads, and we had this chocolate with pistachio swirls—I had three of those—astounding absolutely astounding.

And I had a lots of champagne—that's what I remember. I remember the food was just astounding.

MAURICE: Maybe not everything, but it was impressive. I remember the dessert which was creme brulee. I remember—there were too many things—something with truffles at the beginning. I don't remember the details. Was there something with the truffles? The creme I remember, because we had too much wine and the creme was so delicious and I ate the whole thing, although I didn't think I could finish it because I was so full. There were about five or six dishes—one thing, maybe the first one, was truffles, There was . . . did we have sweetbreads or something? There was fish, I believe. That's all I can remember.

STEVE: I remember we were at Jamin and we had several courses, and enough wine to make me want to lie down which I think I did, and I'm drawing a blank on the food.

It was a really great meal, but my friends didn't really remember it that well. How odd? Don't people remember exciting and unusual events? Why didn't they remember what they had eaten?

> FOOD FOR THOUGHT   *Why didn't my friends remember that really great meal all that well? Don't people remember the details of exciting and unusual events?*

Well, Steve got drunk. That much seems clear. Maurice, who was French and a gourmet, remembered what he was impressed by: the crème brulee. He remembered that there was a lot of food. And he recalled the truffles and sweetbread.

I was also interested in storytelling when I called my friends, so I not only asked them what they ate. I followed by asking them to tell me the story of that night. Here is what Maurice said:

> *"It was a pity because very few people did appreciate the food, maybe three or four of us. But the rest, some of these Americans didn't see that they were having the most fantastic food in the world. They were sort of bitching about the things being fat or salty. They couldn't perceive the odors—the perfumes of the stuff. I think that this was a waste. The invitation was partly wasted—not on friends maybe—but maybe on uneducated guests."*

Maurice did remember the event quite well. He remembered how he felt. But he did not really remember the details of the event, despite having a keen interest in them at the time and being exasperated by the lack of interest of some of the other guests.

What Does This Tell Us About Human Memory?

A great deal if this is not an isolated event in an odd situation. Let's look at what some of the others recalled.

Jerry remembered that were only appetizers and desserts and, besides that, he only remembered the crème brulee.

So Jerry couldn't remember much. Does this mean he wasn't paying attention to the food? Here is what he said in his story of the night:

> *"The thing about it that was most interesting to me was that there were three sets of people involved. There were some Americans, a couple Brits, and the French. The Brits were loud and boisterous and fairly obnoxious. The French*

all sat in one corner and smoked constantly and refused to talk English to anybody, more or less, and looked very superior. I felt fairly embarrassed throughout the whole thing."

So while Jerry may have liked the food, his memory was distracted by the event itself. For him too, the event overwhelmed the details, despite how much he may have enjoyed the details.

Anatole remembered one dish (the lobster ravioli) and the look of one of the desserts. Anatole is Russian born, but has lived in the U.S. most of his adult life. He is very sophisticated about food and has traveled a great deal. He too, had no problem remembering the event:

"It was in this wonderful French restaurant. We had a room on the second floor and it was very rowdy, everybody was reminiscing and paying very little attention to the food and this old French professor was getting more and more sad. As time went by, Laurence [one of the French guests] was getting sadder and sadder because she couldn't believe that people weren't concentrating on this wonderful food. And I remember Jerry Feldman's wife kind of examining every little piece of food on her fork—you know, picking it up and examining it every time. And Laurence getting more and more vindictive and blowing cigarette smoke in their faces. It was almost a riot. But everybody had a wonderful time."

So he too remembered the feelings and the experience. He also remembered that others weren't concentrating on the food.

Andrew (one of above-referenced Brits, although he has lived in the U.S. most of his adult life as well) remembered offal. That is, he had a category for some of our experience that night—which Americans typically do not have—in which sweetbreads and liver fit. He remembered two dishes in other words, probably because he didn't usually eat them (and, one would guess, he didn't much like them).

> *"There were several things that stick out in my memory about it. In sequence, we were led up to this magnificent private room and the first thing that happened that I recall was that there was someone there who was a waiter who was serving champagne. And there were glasses of champagne on the tray. And I recall vividly that he spilled somehow a glass or two on the floor and managed to get it all over Jerry Feldman's wife. That struck me as humorous because it was so improbable in that context. One's expectation was that these people had done these things a thousand times and it was not very likely that they would spill the wine, spill the champagne, and even less likely that they would spill it over one of the clients—I remember that very vividly. And then we all sat down around this long table and I recall that I knew about three-fourths of the people and the people that I didn't know I had just met the day before. They were the French people mainly. And then we started this meal with multiple courses, with a different wine for most, if not all of the courses.*
>
> *"I remember then that my wife isn't used to eating . . . the kinds of food that we had and also she found there to be a hell of a lot of this food. Also, she wasn't used to drinking as much wine as she was being provided. One's glass was constantly being filled up and the next thing I remember is that she would eat, on the average, about half of what was on her plate. She was sitting next to Elliot, who has an infinite capacity. So she would pass on to Elliot what she couldn't eat and he had no problem with eating it all. . . . Nor could she accommodate the amount of wine she was*

being served so she passed that on to Steve. And only three courses of the way through the meal did she realize that this was a self-defeating proposition because as soon as she emptied her glass . . . [it] was immediately refilled. So the next vivid memory was that as this meal went on, Elliot became increasingly stuffed because he'd had 50 percent more than anyone else at the table. Steve became increasingly drunk because he had 50 percent more to drink than anyone at the table.

"Then, at the completion of the meal, I recall that brandy and cigars were served. . . . It was all very jolly and great fun. That's basically my recollection of the evening."

Andrew's evening did not really revolve around the food, so of course, he didn't remember it very well. He remembered how his wife annoyed him (he got divorced a few years later), and he remembered Elliot eating and Steve drinking. The event overrode the food.

Elliot is a friend who is more of a gourmand than a gourmet. He can eat me under the table any day (and I can eat a lot). So shouldn't Elliot have remembered what he ate? No. He remembered that he ate a lot and he remembered why. Here is Elliot's story:

"We had a birthday party with incredible individuals—the most interesting people in the field at the most incredible restaurant in Paris, France. And we had food that was just beyond belief and we had eight courses of it and it was just astounding. I sat next to two women who were on diets so I had three of everything, so I was in complete seventh heaven. It was an evening that you don't have very often—that's how I would describe it. Actually, I described it like that."

There really is no surprise here. Why would he remember what he ate? It wasn't the fun part for him. He just remembered liking what he ate.

Don didn't remember what he ate at all. I found this odd as Don is a very detail-oriented psychologist who can recall many details of events he has experienced and who I know loves good food. When I asked Don for a story about what happened that evening, this is the core of what he said:

> *"I recall being ushered upstairs into a private room. I recall that there was a vast array of champagne to start with—champagne that I thought was donated by somebody. We then sat down—it was a fairly formal setting, not that any of the guests were formal. We had menus—not menus but a list of what it is that we are going to receive.*
>
> *"I would estimate that I knew half the participants. I can't recall much of the dinner itself, that is, the eating, except that it was a wide variety of foods, relatively small in portion—I think Roger announced that that was the proper way to eat rather than stuff yourself with a large amount of one thing, you should have a sampling of many such things. I also recall being in full agreement. The meal was typically high cuisine French, that is, it was elegant with rich sauces, relatively textureless where the sauces dominated, and the texture of the food was sometimes deliberately invisible. I remember various speeches and goodwill. Its hard to remember what else there was except a good time was had by all and if asked to attend another one I would, even though my memory for it seems to be so incredibly poor."*

So was my dinner a waste of time and food? Wasn't it sad that no one remembered what they ate? We may as well have been at McDonald's. At least they would have remembered the food.

Actually I don't find it sad at all. What would be sad would be a situation where a big event was organized that was intended to make sure that people remembered the details of their experience that was easily forgotten. Like, for example, a training event.

WHAT IF THE TRAINING YOU DO WERE LIKE THIS?

Why would your training events be remembered any differently than my birthday dinner was remembered? Think about what the participants at my dinner did remember.

They remembered their *feelings* at the time. They remembered *having fun*. They remembered the *behavior of others*. They remembered things that they found personally exciting or disgusting. They remembered *who annoyed them, who interested them, and they remembered being embarrassed.*

What happens at a training event? Lots of people come together and have a mutual experience. They laugh, maybe they cry. They feel uncomfortable or embarrassed. If they have fun, they remember having fun. If they are bored or unhappy, they remember that. But they will forget the details, just as my friends did. More, since the details of your training event are likely to be a lot less interesting or enjoyable.

My dinner wasn't particularly exceptional or weird (except for the food). It was a typical human event. People met. They interacted. Things happened. Feelings were felt. And that was what was remembered. First and foremost it is always the feelings that are remembered. And of course, the conclusions, the attitudes, and the reactions can be recalled as well.

> *What do people remember? Their feelings. Fun. The behavior of others. What they don't remember are the details—they are not the important stuff of human memory.*

The details? Even when they are absolutely fascinating; even when they are tremendously unusual; even when they are the best of their kind in the world, they will be forgotten. Details cannot remain under these circumstances. They are not the important stuff of human memory.

What Does This Tell Us About Training?

First, it tells us that if you organize training events hoping that your trainees will learn the details of something, any details at all, you will be greatly disappointed. Spend two days showing PowerPoint® slides about company policies, or how to do something on a computer, or the proper way to manage employees, and what people will remember is the cute guy sitting next to them or how embarrassed they were by what they wore or who sounded cool when he spoke. Or if a speaker did something funny to illustrate a point they will remember what he did. They will, however, likely forget the point he was illustrating.

Are all training events doomed in this way?

Yes.

> *If a speaker does something funny to illustrate a point, people will remember what he did. They will, however, likely forget the point he was illustrating.*

I know this is hard to swallow. Thousands of companies have spent billions of dollars on training events and here I am saying all this money is totally wasted?

Well, no.

People meet people at these events and this is a good thing. You should know the folks you work with and training events are sometimes good ways to meet and get to know people. People are sometimes inspired by such events or by a person who speaks at one of these events. They may not recall what he said exactly, but, as they remember feelings and their reactions to people, they are likely to stay inspired, at least for a while.

But they will not be trained at training events. It can't happen. Human beings simply cannot remember the details in a complex social situation very well. You can hope they will remember, but they simply cannot.

> *Human beings simply cannot remember the details in a complex social situation very well.*

Then under what circumstances will they be trained, you ask?

To answer this we must again think about human memory. Specifically, we need to understand . . .

The Difference Between Event Memory and Procedural Memory

Try to remember a birthday party that was given in your honor, or a similar event you might have attended. Does your memory differ wildly in type from those you saw presented here? Do you remember every detail of what you ate? Certain events may stand out, but its mostly people and your feelings you recall, right?

Now try to remember learning a skill that you now know well. For example, you might know how to hit a baseball. Do you remember learning to do it? Or you might know how to sew. Do you remember learning to do it? Or take a mental skill rather than a physical one. Did you ever learn to program a computer or solve a differential equation?

Do you remember the event of learning to do these things? Perhaps you do. Perhaps you remember who taught you or how you felt about the experience. But, and this is the important part, if you recall your first stabs at doing these skills, what you are remembering is the event of learning. The skills themselves, the procedures you learned to follow when you first learned, can likely be barely recalled at all.

> *If you recall your first stabs at learning to sew, or hit a baseball, or program a computer, and such, what you are remembering is the event of learning. The skills themselves, the procedures you learned to follow when you first learned, can likely be barely recalled at all.*

Why is this? *Because you have practiced them many times since.* The first time was simply the first time, when you were awkward and unsure of yourself. After hundreds of attempts, you got better and those initial awkward attempts have nothing to do with what you now know. What you know has been reinforced by practice. As an expert you can cite odd experiences when things didn't work as planned, but the basics are so ingrained in you that you hardly know that you know them. You simply know how to execute them. It doesn't matter what you first did or thought on your first attempts at these things. Once you have learned a skill you no longer need to retain the initial false starts. Memory for procedures isn't like memory for events. It needn't keep the details around. How-to memory consists of a set of steps not a set of events.

Procedures, and Thus Procedural Memory, Can Only Be Learned by Practice

What this means in effect is that for procedural memory, training that is not about repetition of experience and endless repetition at that, is a waste of time.

> *Memory for procedures isn't like memory for events. It needn't keep the details around. How-to memory consists of a set of steps not a set of events.*

When I was planning my fortieth birthday menu, I remembered the truffle dish because I had practiced eating it. (The practicing was great fun, of course.) I had eaten it a number of times and over time the details became more salient. If I had wanted my friends to remember the food, I would have had to repeat the exact dinner three or four times. With practice they would have retained the details. They too would have enjoyed the practice, although I suspect they would have rebelled after a bit.

To put this another way—a way that may be unpalatable for many of you—classrooms are, for the most part, a waste of time.

You Cannot Learn Anything in a Classroom That Is Procedural in Nature

In other words, you can't learn to do anything in a passive classroom setting where a speaker speaks and everyone else listens or asks the occasional question. You can be told about doing things, but in that case you are experiencing an event and you will remember as much of that event as my friends remembered of my dinner. That is, not much.

If You Want People to Learn to Do Something, You Must Have Them Do It, and Do It Repeatedly

Unless there is a way that they can practice in the classroom, little learning can possibly take place there. Events will be remembered, however. Everyone remembers how he or she felt in the classroom. They remember who was there and what the experience was like. They simply will not, because they cannot, remember the details.

My friends were invited back when I was fifty. Not to Paris but to a great restaurant in Chicago, where I was living at the time, where the chef agreed with my small portions and lots of different stuff to taste approach to eating. None of the wives who had come to Paris attended. They had all been divorced by that time. There was a lot more going on than the food. There always is.

◊   ◊   ◊

Jump Start Your Thinking

What You Remember from an Event
• Feelings
• Visual images

- People
- Unexpected situations and their resolution

HOW TO MAKE USE OF THIS INFORMATION IN TRAINING

- Make trainees feel something—fear; exhilaration; surprise; happiness; any feeling will do (except boredom).

- Make sure trainees see things (other than PowerPoint slides); these should be unusual things that cause them to wonder about them; smells work here as well.

- Insist on many varied interactions between people; these are best if they are one-on-one interactions that involve dealing with some real issue.

- Make sure that something that is truly unexpected happens and that the point you want to drive home in training is illuminated by that unusual event.

8

Sir, Step Away from the Fig Newton

HOW WHAT HAPPENS IN REAL LIFE UNDOES TRAINING— AND WHAT TO DO ABOUT IT

I was selected to be "wanded" after going through the metal detector at the airport the other day. The uniformed man did the usual "put your arms out" routine and then noticed a bulge in my pocket. "What's that?" he said. "A Fig Newton," said I. He made me take it out and put it on the table. I must say I am very impressed with security at the airports these days. No one will be hijacking any planes using a Fig Newton, that's for sure.

"What does this have to do with training?" you wonder.

Well, everything, as it turns out. Bear with me . . .

While trying to help my kids select a path in life, I always encouraged them to follow their hearts. My son was a subway nut—he felt the need to ride every line of every subway he encountered in any city he visited. So I encouraged him to study transportation when he got to college, and he did. He got a job, while in graduate school, working for the New York subway system and was as happy as a pig in mud. Eventually he expanded his horizons and he went to work for the U.S. Department of Transportation. This was just prior to 9/11/2001. So despite the fact that he had learned to be a theorist about transportation in graduate school, he one day found himself smuggling guns, knives, and bombs through metal detectors and human wanders, and onto airplanes. He was doing this because DOT has some worries about the vulnerability of the system, as do we all. I am sorry to say that the results of what he has been doing won't make you worry any less. He got more stuff through than he cared to say. When I told him about the Fig Newton, he had a pretty good explanation for what was going on.

He said that the guys who do the wanding never find much besides keys and spare change, so in a sense, that is what they look for. They examine what is in your pockets because it is a kind of success. "Oh boy, I found something." They feel a kind of satisfaction when they find some metal because they feel like they have been doing their jobs and you have been found out. (Okay, maybe the Fig Newton didn't give the guy very much satisfaction, but those nail clippers are probably pretty exciting.)

What does this have to do with training, you ask?

Everything.

How Is It Possible to Teach Somebody to Do Something if That Something Never Happens?

This question is more important than it appears to be at first glance. For years we have been training people about what to do in a catastrophe and that training has always seemed odd at best. I am from the era when we all hid under our desks in school, making sure to point our rear ends toward the window, in case of nuclear attack. Believe me, it doesn't just seem funny in retrospect, it made no sense to any ten-year-old I knew at the time.

Adults are trained to watch for earthquakes, or melt downs at power plants, or any number of things that never happen, so how do we train people to do the right thing when the "once in a blue moon" finally actually happens?

Remember, as we think about this, that people learn best by practice. You want to play the violin—practice. You want to be good at giving speeches—practice. You want to be a good parent—practice. Ah, whoops—about that last one. Who do you practice on? You see that's the problem. While most people do practice on their first child and get way better with grandchildren, in general this is not a great strategy.

So How do We Practice When What We Want to Practice Is Impossible to Practice?

I bet you think I am going to say computer simulations because you might know that I have been building those for years. Actually, I'm not going to talk about simulations. What I am worrying about here is all those places where computer simulations either wouldn't work or would be way too hard or too expensive to build. How do we practice that stuff?

What might training for baggage screeners and human wanders look like, for example? If they were taught to look for stuff that was in unusual places in their training they might become very proficient at knowing where to look and what to do. We could do that with a computer simulation or we could do it with live subjects like my son. But, and this is the real issue: that training would be undone by reality. Yes, my son was carrying a gun, but how often does that happen? Training continues throughout real life whether the trainers like it or not. It does not occur solely in training (or in school). You can teach anyone anything you like, drum it into their heads by repeated testing, and it will go right out again if it isn't used. More importantly, the training will actually be undone, reversed in effect, by a trainee discovering that what he has learned brings no rewards or that the real rewards are elsewhere.

> *Training continues throughout real life whether the trainers like it or not.*

This is, of course, exactly what goes on in school all the time. Train people to do geometry all you want, spend the whole tenth grade at it if you like. It really doesn't matter because they will never do it again, and it will be forgotten until the day they try to recollect it when their kids need help with their homework. (Of course, this makes one wonder why anyone ever learns geometry, but that is a subject for a different essay.) Train them on the subjunctive case in French all you want, they may even pass the French placement exam using that information, but when they arrive in France, the reality of speaking in simple sentences just to get anyone to understand you at all will untrain them from worrying about proper grammar, by focussing their attention on recalling the word for "undercooked."

The same is true with airport security.

QUESTION: HOW THEN SHOULD WE TRAIN
PEOPLE WHEN WE KNOW THAT REALITY WILL
UNTRAIN THEM?

Ten hours of proper procedure training will be undone by a thousand hours of "no one ever brings a gun with them anyway." There is more than one answer to this question. The first relates to school:

Answer #1. Stop training people for things they will never do

In real life almost no one does logarithms, writes essays about their summer vacation, needs to recount important events in U.S. history, compares the work of Dickens with the works of Tolstoy, or balances a chemical equation. These things never come up, so no matter how much you may have enjoyed them (or not) in high school, they are soon forgotten. Moreover, they should be forgotten, because they don't matter. Excuses like learning things like this helps you learn to learn, or learn to reason, or introduces you to things you might want to do in the future, are simply unproven and most likely untrue. Our whole school system rests on assumptions like these, and they are very likely wrong assumptions. It is still a radical idea in education circles to try teaching what people are going to need when they go out into the real world. What will new adults entering the real world need? Why not look around and see what people do in the real world? I am not the first to suggest this. No one paid much attention when Ben Franklin said the same things in 1754. (Or for that matter when Plato said them whenever he said them.)

> *What will new adults entering the real world need? Why not look around and see what people do in the real world?*

And what if what we train people to do doesn't correspond to what they actually do? Or to what they are going to do? What if we can't really teach them something because what we teach will be undone by the events of their daily lives?

To answer this, let me tell you a story. I was once asked by the Dutch government to help them teach teenagers not to smoke. I suggested that they create a biology curriculum for high schools that involved having students work in a simulated lung cancer laboratory for a year dealing with diseased tissues and real patients on video who were dying from lung cancer. I figured that most lung cancer doctors don't smoke, and that after a year in this simulated lab neither would the teenagers (and they might learn a little real biology on the way). This was too radical for the government, as you might imagine, who just wanted to "say no to cigarettes" in a multimedia format.

Why would the lung cancer lab simulation work? Because people are emotional beings and they remember emotional experiences. School and training are eminently forgettable because they are usually unemotional (except of course for the fear of failing). But seeing sickening stuff day in and day out for a year can cause a heavy resolve to be created that enables people to resist the realities of the outside world (like that all their friends smoke). In other words, the reward system (peer approval, or finding a nail clipper) is replaced by a deeper emotional bias that is not easily undone because it has been placed inside one's psyche.

So, that having been said: how do we train airport security people? By scaring the hell out of them, that's how. By having them go into their wanding act so frightened of what they might fail to find that they actually look where their emotions take them, not where the reward system takes them.

Answer #2. Train people for things that they will never encounter by kindling deep emotional reactions

And how do we do that?

I have always admired the Department of Motor Vehicles. They usually seem to get it right about learning. They have two tests they administer in order to get a driver's license. One is the usual silly multiple-choice test that tests whether you can temporarily memorize a bunch of useless facts. But after that, they actually test to see whether you can drive the car! Think about the brilliance of this. The schools almost never do the same. They don't test to see if you can do biology. They don't even know what that would mean. They just see if you can memorize some facts about biology.

So what should we be doing in order to train airport screeners? One wonders how many of them have talked to or heard from or seen an interview with the screeners who were on duty in Boston, New York, and Washington on 9/11/2001. Funny how you don't hear about them. I can see many reasons not to vilify them and hold them up to ridicule. But on the other hand, I can see no reason why their feelings and their rehash of what happened, which certainly must plague them, is not part of every training program for airport security.

This brings up a larger issue, of course. There are things that simply never have happened. And for those things, training is nearly impossible. But for those things that happen infrequently, where only a few people have had relevant experiences, it is vital that those experiences be made available to trainees. Now, bear in mind that those experience are quite often going to be experiences about bad events. In other words, we need to record mistakes, disasters, stories about traumatic experiences, and make these required viewing (or listening) for trainees.

> *To train people for things that they are likely to never encounter we need to record mistakes, disasters, stories about traumatic experiences, and make these required viewing (or listening).*

Such stories may not be easy to elicit, but it has to be done. They may also not be easy to watch, but that too has to be done. And since simply listening is not the best way to learn, they may not be easy to re-live, but somehow that has to be done as well. Airport screeners should really know what it feels like to have screwed the screening up. This is the emotional component and it is very important in any learning situation.

But the emotional component is not all there is.

The last answer to how to teach people to do what they never actually do, is teaching people to comprehend their own goals.

Answer #3. Train people for things that they will never encounter by changing the reward system

So airport screeners almost never see a gun, but they do encounter the occasional Fig Newton. More importantly they find coins, and keys, and cell phones on a regular basis. How do they feel when they find these things? Well, pretty good, one would assume. They have done their job. They were supposed to find these things. If they hadn't they would have messed up. So they are rewarded every time they find them. How can we change this?

When the rewards screw up learning you need to change the reward system. When students are rewarded by A's they learn that getting A's is what school is all about. I have been a professor for thirty-five years and I can tell you that students are so grade-oriented that they will argue and complain about any grade they get. They don't worry about what they have learned; they feel they are doing well in school if they are getting good grades. Sometimes it doesn't seem that learning is in their sights at all. College is about parties, sex, alcohol, and grades.

> *When the rewards screw up learning, you need to change the reward system.*

The same sort of thing is going on with the airport screeners. I am not suggesting that they are in it for the parties or the beer, but the reward part is the same. It is a good day if they got their rewards. This means finding lots of keys. How do we change this? Change the reward system. They are trying to find potential hijackers after all. So we need to reward them when they find one. Someone who still has his keys in his pocket is not a potential hijacker. If the equipment they are using is so primitive that it can't tell a Fig Newton from a knife, then we can only fix this by training people to look for different things. They should look for hijackers.

How can they do that? The problem is that there aren't very many hijackers. (I realize that this isn't really a problem, but it is a problem for the reward system.) The answer is obvious then: make more hijackers.

Suppose that three times a day someone tries to come through the metal detector with an object taped to his leg or hidden in an odd place. Suppose that the wanders had to find those people every day and that that was their real reward. If they found them they felt good about themselves and were seen as doing their job. If not, their jobs would be in jeopardy. They would be unlikely to be excited about finding the occasional nail clipper in that case. Short of hiring my son to endlessly do this smuggling job, it would be much easier to ask actual passengers to participate. Many would gladly do this, seeing it as civic duty. This has the advantage that the screeners would be dealing with actual people rather than with government employees. Most importantly, the reward system would be changed. The wanders would go to work looking for knife smugglers and not Fig Newton eaters.

The message here is simple:

If you want to train people to do something for which the reward system is screwed up, you must change the reward system.

Otherwise what happens in real life will undo the training every time. And if you want to train people to deal with situations in which failure can be catastrophic, then making them constantly emotionally connected to the catastrophes that have happened has great value.

◊ ◊ ◊

Jump Start Your Training

More Do's and Don'ts
- Don't have trainees practice for events that almost never happen.

- Don't establish rewards that undermine the training.
- Don't build a simulation for events that hardly ever occur.
- Do realize that training is taking place all the time, not only during a training session.
- Do train for what really will happen on the job.
- Do train people not to do something by giving them emotional reasons not to.
- Do train people for things that hardly ever happen by kindling deep emotional reactions when they do.
- Do use the emotional experiences of your employees in the form of stories told at appropriate places during training.
- Do encourage the telling of disaster stories.
- Do train people for things that rarely happen by concentrating on changing the reward system.
- Do create live simulations that look and feel real.
- Do find ways to build in the experience of people who have "been there."

9

Billy's Home Run

STORYTELLING INSIGHTS—AND HOW HEARING, TELLING,
AND LIVING STORIES MAKES FOR GOOD TRAINING

I play softball with a bunch of old guys (I am no longer so young myself) who have little else to do. They are all retired and softball is pretty much the highlight of their day. So they take it rather seriously. They were, for the most part, great athletes who are now operating on less than 100 percent of what they used to be. They can still hit, and they often field pretty well too.

Billy is sixty-five years old. He had a heart attack when he was quite young, so he takes very good care of himself. He also plays a mean center field. Despite his years he is still very fast. He is a little guy though, so when he hits the ball over an outfielder's head it is an unusual event. But on a blistering hot July day, he did just that.

Our team was rooting for him as he rounded second. He was going real fast and it looked like he could get a home run as the left fielder was just getting to the ball at that point. "Go, Billy," everyone yelled from the bench. "You can make it, Billy." "Atta boy, Billy." Then, suddenly someone yelled, "Don't die, Billy!"

Billy stopped at third. He could have made it home. Seemed like a good choice to me.

A large part of our lives is taken up by the telling of stories. We tell stories to our friends about our exploits, travel adventures, odd work experiences, things our children did, and so on. Teachers tell stories that illustrate points they want to make. Old people tell the same stories over and over again. But we usually don't think much about where those stories come from or why we think they are worth telling or what the telling says about who we are.

> *A large part of our lives is taken up by the telling of stories. But we usually don't think much about where those stories come from or why we think they are worth telling or what the telling says about who we are.*

Billy was choosing between stories. Like most everyone who lives with someone and arrives home after doing something somewhere else, he was going to tell the story of his morning to his wife. We all knew that he wanted to tell the "I hit a home run" story to his wife. In fact, we can imagine that telling this story was going to be the highlight of his week, maybe his year. But for a moment, perhaps responding to the "don't die" remark, he thought about the "we regret to inform you" story that someone might be instead telling his wife later that morning. He chose the "I almost hit a home run but was prudent" story. Not as much fun to be sure, but he would be there to tell it.

Or at least I thought he had made that choice. I was curious, so I asked him. He said, "There was nobody out, so I was sure that I would be scoring anyway from third, so why push it?" I thought that odd so I asked him again the next day about the incident and he again told that same story. He just couldn't bring himself to say that he was worried about dying. He admitted it when I pressed him on it, but then went back to his preferred "prudent softball player" story.

We define ourselves through the stories we choose to tell. What we tell isn't always what exactly happened, however. We embellish. We smooth out the rough edges. We get rid of the stuff we aren't proud of. We tell a story that makes us feel happy to tell it. We tell stories that fit within our conceptions of ourselves.

This all has a profound effect on what we see as truth. The stories people tell are those stories that they choose to tell because they make themselves look the way they want to be seen. And decisions are sometimes made because we want to be able to tell a particular story. We eat at a great restaurant because we want to say we ate there and tell about how great it is, even though we didn't really want to spend all that money and don't like great food that well. Not me, of course. I love great restaurants, but you get the idea.

To put this in another context: while the use of stories in business—and especially in training—is critical, you have to realize that *what you hear isn't always what actually happened.* You need to look closely at the stories. Some stories are told because what they describe happened that way, but for the most part there are many ways to see an event or a series of events. And there are times we do things simply because we like the story that we can tell afterward. Similarly, there are things we don't do because we don't think the story will sell well, even though we think it is the right thing to do.

> *The use of stories in business—and especially in training— is critical, but what you hear isn't always what actually happened.*

Politicians are, of course, constantly rewriting their stories. Whenever an error is made, a scapegoat is found. Suddenly the story being told revolves around the errors made by the scapegoat. After a while people stop looking for what really happened and begin to base their opinions around the story that is being told. "Should we invade Iraq to attempt to control the region?" becomes "Let's search for weapons of mass destruction." The real story doesn't sell so well, so politicians tell a story that will sell better. We all see this when we watch the evening news. Storytelling and, more importantly, story selling, is a politician's specialty.

But what about in business? Is the same thing happening?

What About the Stories We Tell in Training?

How real are they?

Companies love to tell official stories. As I noted in Chapter 2, these official stories are quite often entirely irrelevant to any experience employees are likely to have.

An Example of How Official Stories Work

Recently someone gave me a motorcycle. So I found myself reading the motorcycle handbook put out by the state of

Florida in order to pass the test to get a permit. There are, of course, sample test questions. Here is one:

TEST YOUR KNOWLEDGE

> 14. *If you wait an hour for each drink before riding:*
>
> A. *you cannot be arrested for drinking and riding.*
>
> B. *your riding skills will not be affected.*
>
> C. *side effects from the drinking may still remain.*
>
> D. *you will be okay as long as you ride slowly.*

Of course, I didn't bother to read what the State of Florida said was true about this. It didn't matter what the truth actually might be either. Anyone who sees this type of question knows full well that not drinking before driving is going to be the right answer. So the real questions remain. How safe is it to drink, wait an hour, and then drive? This is something you might actually want to know, but the State of Florida won't tell you that. It will only tell you the official story. So naturally, we have all learned to ignore the official stories that governments tell and to be skeptical of any story we hear from a politician.

This leaves us with the question of what stories we believe. As I pointed out earlier, even Billy didn't necessarily believe Billy's story, although it is fair to say that as time goes on he will believe it more. Billy doesn't want to think about dying.

So Whose Stories Do We Believe?

This is a question that is very important for any trainer.

As I have been saying for years, stories are critical for comprehension. Stories are all we remember. Our intelligence is made up of stories. Story exchange is what conversation is all about. Stories are at the center of our ability to understand the world around us. Nevertheless, we don't believe the vast majority of the stories we hear.

> *Stories are critical for comprehension, yet we don't believe the vast majority of the stories we hear.*

When you decide to put your CEO on as the first video clip of a multimedia production—don't bother. No one will listen. And no one will believe what he says if by mistake they happen to actually hear any of it. Now I know this is difficult to accept. Just think about what these guys actually say: *At XYZ corporation we put our faith in our employees. We know that happy employees make happy customers. So we invest time in educating you and your family . . . blah blah blah.*

Does anyone listen to this junk? Why does anyone bother saying it? Do they actually believe it? Why do CEOs insist on saying it? They like thinking it is true I suppose. Or maybe they just like their own voices so much that truth doesn't enter into it.

So what do people believe, then? What will they listen to? This is easy. They believe stories that are not rationalizations or self-justifications or bland statements of the obvious. That is why when they really want to teach you not to drink and drive they show you videos of dead people in car accidents. If the CEO told a story about how he really screwed up big time by making a decision that he was never going to make again, the audience would believe the "screwed up big time" part and would be skeptical of the "I won't do it again" part. But at least they would have heard something. *People believe each other's emotional pain.*

STORYTELLING BASICS

People won't believe . . .

- Rationalization
- Self-justification
- Restatement of the blindingly obvious

People will believe . . .

- Someone else's emotional pain

One problem with stories is that, while they often describe what happened, they also are the reason that something happened. I can remember deciding to stay in college, when I really wanted to quit for a while. I didn't want that to be my story, I didn't want be judged by that story, I didn't want to have to tell my children not to do what I did. I was quite aware that I was creating my own story and I made decisions based on what story I was going to have to tell.

When Billy was deciding to stop at third, he was choosing between stories (even if he didn't explicitly think that). This is what happens to us on a regular basis in life, and not surprisingly, in the workplace as well. It is within the story selection process that interesting things happen.

Suppose you have to decide whether to pursue a risky path in a business situation. In making the decision of whether or not to pursue this path, you decide (again implicitly—this is not a conscious process) between competing stories. You tell yourself the "hero story"—how you chose the risky path and, against all odds, won. You tell yourself the "goat story"—how you thought you'd take a chance and all right it didn't work out but it seemed like a good idea at the time. And you also tell yourself the "do nothing" story, the good company man who takes no risks and simply does his job. And you decide the relative impact on you of living with these stories.

Now here is the odd part: The hero story may not sound so good and the do nothing story may not sound so bad. It depends on the world you live in. In some companies, the hero story doesn't actually work. Some companies really abhor risk, and even when it works out they wonder about the guy who was willing to take it. And similarly, some companies rather like the company guy who takes no chances. They like the team player who doesn't rock the boat.

So an important question for trainers is . . .

WHICH TYPE OF STORIES DOES YOUR COMPANY ENCOURAGE ITS PEOPLE TO LIVE OUT?

To put this another way, wouldn't it be the proper concern for training to attempt to remedy broken cultures? Cultures that encourage doing nothing to force change tend to produce negative results. What stories do people choose to live (and therefore to tell) because the surrounding culture encourages it?

> THE "STANDARDS" STORY   *One of my favorite stories that define a culture belongs to the academic world in which I live. It is what I call the "standards" story. The standards story is invoked, with holy righteousness, every time someone tries to make a change that might cause more work for the faculty. Recently, I was attempting to get some students admitted into graduate school who seemed perfectly qualified to me but yet had been rejected by the faculty in their subject area. The reason given was that the applicants did not have sufficient work experience. They were to be told that they should go to work for two years and then apply again. I asked what these students would learn from their two years' work experience and was given a list of good things that would happen to them in an ideal world.*

I suggested that, as things didn't always go the way one might hope out there in the real world, perhaps we could construct a simulation of the work experience that would serve to teach the very things the faculty thought these students would learn while working. (This is not all that odd a suggestion because we use a curriculum that is entirely a simulation of work situations in any case. We do not have classes or lectures in our curriculum.)

The faculty said that, although this could be done, it would be a case of "lowering standards." Ah, the old "lowering standards" story. Faculty love that story. They tell it any time they might have to do some more work. It is such a lovely story. So sanctimonious, so full of self-righteousness and self-love. We are the greatest, the story goes. Students should kill to get in here. We only take the best. We would never take less than the best, because that would lower the quality of the whole institution. Everyone would suffer.

I always wonder about this story. If everyone you take is a superstar after all, it doesn't take much effort to teach them. When geniuses enter your Ph.D. program they tend to come out geniuses. Quel suprise!

A good teacher takes pride in helping a non-genius become a competent, functioning professional. A good teacher takes pride in helping a genius who has not shown herself to be a genius to achieve all she can achieve. But you have to lower standards to admit such problem cases. Or to put this another way, you might have to do some real work. And, sad to say, most professors do not consider working with students to be their actual calling. So they keep standards up.

One story that great universities want to tell, for example, is the "how hard it is to get in here" story. As it turns out, this story is much less true in general than people think. Oh sure, it is real hard to get into Harvard as an undergraduate, but I am sure Harvard has graduate programs that are not all that difficult to get into. Yale certainly does (in this, I speak from experience).

Most colleges are rather easy to get into, actually, but you can be sure they don't advertise that fact. The "hard to get into" story makes all those associated with a college feel that much better about themselves. Unfortunately, this particular story isn't real good for education in general. The storytellers don't care. They are more concerned with how good it makes them feel to tell the story.

Meanwhile, back in your training department . . . everything I have said to this point has been to jog your thinking about how stories shape the way we understand the world around us.

WHAT SHOULD YOU KNOW, THEN, WHEN USING STORIES IN TRAINING?

- First: use real stories.
- Second: never tell without using a story.
- Third: make sure the tellers are authentic.
- Fourth: make sure the tellers don't blandify the story.
- Fifth: include the "story choice" as part of the story.
- Sixth: tell only those stories that can be heard.
- Seventh: tell stories just in time.
- Eighth: recognize that story living is better than story telling.
- Ninth: surprise your listener.
- Tenth: remember Billy.

Use Real Stories

What is a real story? Something you would tell your friends about your day at work. Or if the CEO is telling it, then something he would tell his friends about his day at work. Do not bother ever saying anything in training that isn't real. Trainees detect the lack of reality in a New York minute. All stories must be ones that were not specially constructed for the training.

> *Don't bother ever saying anything in training that isn't real.*

People have good BS detectors. Stop testing them. Once they hear one official story they disbelieve even the ones that are real. So make sure that your company is choosing good stories in the first place, before the telling.

Never Tell Without Using a Story

So if you can only use real stories, how can you say the stuff that people just have to know that doesn't fit in the form of a story?

Good question.

Answer: don't even think about telling it to them.

Trainers need to learn that telling doesn't work. Do you hear me? Are you listening? Will you do what I say? No. Why not?

Because telling doesn't work.

Stories, stories, stories. If you want to make a point, use a story that makes that point. And then use another.

When I am trying to convince people that telling doesn't work, I give them a quiz about airline safety, the answers to which are all contained in those horribly boring videos they show before every flight that everyone tunes out at the part where they tell you how to fasten your seat belt. (Talk about a dumb way to start a training video: *Tell them something that everyone already knows, that'll get them to pay attention!*)

> *If you want to make a point, use a story that makes that point. And then use another.*

And, you know what? No one that I ask, and I mean no one, can answer simple questions like "How many life rafts are there and where are they located?" despite the fact that they have heard this information countless times.

Why is that? Because you can't learn from being told. No one pays attention, or if they do, they immediately forget what they heard. A funny story about trying to find the life raft (or maybe a terribly unfunny one) would certainly have helped.

Just don't tell official stories. No one is listening.

Make Sure the Tellers Are Authentic

What makes an authentic teller?

Someone who is real is authentic. Don't use actors. Don't use people who never actually do the job they are telling you how to do. Have real people tell real stories in real language. If the real people aren't good storytellers, coach them so that they can become good storytellers. We know when we are hearing a real story. And in a not too large company, we may actually know the guy who is telling the story. This matters more than you would know.

> *Have real people tell real stories in real language.*

Why?

Because our memories depend on indexing to retrieve stories. We need lots of labels to add to what we hear to know where to place the stuff we have heard in our memories. (This is not a conscious process. I don't actually mean we are consciously trying to put things in memory locations. But that is what we do.) Indexing on face is good, but it is better if we know the face or have heard of the guy who is speaking. The more we think about what we are hearing, the more indices we can construct to get the information we have just heard. We can't recall the airplane safety video because we aren't thinking about it for even a millisecond.

Make Sure the Tellers Don't Blandify the Story

Pardon my making up a word here, but sometimes English doesn't have all the words it needs. Companies love to blandify. Any time they can sugar coat what they say, or take out the actual names or circumstances, and especially the really bad parts, they will. Unfortunately, the bad parts are just the stuff that people latch onto. It is what they remember. It is what helps them find the story later when they need it.

> *Reality is really good for storytelling. The more bland you make it, the more forgettable it becomes.*

Now, of course, a story about sexual harassment that names names would be better remembered than some blandified version, but there are legal reasons not to do that. Apart from legal or ethical considerations, though, reality is good for storytelling. The gory emotional parts, the "it really screwed up business" parts are important to tell.

The more bland you make it, the more forgettable it becomes. Remember that the next time you tell a story that you hope someone will be able to use later.

Include the "Story Choice" as Part of the Story

Now you had to have been paying attention to know what I am talking about here. People constantly make choices long before they tell a story of the event they are describing—that is, in essence how the story came to take place in the first place. Every story has within it an implicit (and sometimes very explicit) choice. Billy chose to live. Billy chose to tell the "stopping on third because it was the right thing to do for the team" story. But Billy also chose the story he wanted to live (the "I am still alive" or "I am a prudent human being" story). Or maybe I chose to tell that story. Or maybe, even after asking him a couple of times, I still don't know what Billy was really thinking.

> *We choose the stories we want to tell, and that choice is part of the story. In many ways, it is the only part of the story that matters at all.*

The point is, we choose the stories we want to tell. That choice is part of the story. Do not let your experts tell stories in training that leave out the choices they made to get to the point where the story could be told. The choices are critical. In many ways they are the only part of the story that matters at all. They are often explicit within the story ("this is the decision I had to make"). But they are also implicit. Billy's overt choice was triple or home run. His implicit choice was life or death. He told one story. I told the other. Both were true. Things are rarely so black and white.

There are many stories within a story, including why it was chosen to be told at all. Make sure as many stories come out of a story as possible. Yet again, the more that is there, the more that is remembered.

Tell Only Those Stories That Can Be Heard

I could tell my story about Billy to an audience of little leaguers, or for that matter big leaguers, and they wouldn't get it. In fact, in this medium, I have no idea who my readers are and can be pretty sure that it will resonate with some of you and not with others. I have actually told this story to many people, and the results are simple enough to interpret. Men of my age or older who play ball really understand this story. You can see it in their eyes. Others get it less clearly.

For you to understand a story, it must relate to goals you have and experiences you have had. If it relates to both, you will think, "That was the greatest movie I ever saw" or "What a terrific speaker that guy is."

> *What happens when a story relates to both your goals and experiences? You reaction is something like, "That's the greatest thing I ever heard!"*

In general, we understand what we hear when it matches an experience we have had. Everything else is hard to understand. Until you have a pain in your chest from running, you will never quite get the Billy story.

Tell Stories Just in Time

This is more of a hope than a guideline that you can easily implement. Stories must be told just in time, at the moment they are needed, when people are having trouble and need help, when people are willing to listen.

That is all well and good. For years I have been building simulations that utilize just-in-time storytelling, but apart from simulations and just happening to be there when the trouble happens, just-in-time storytelling isn't all that easy to pull off. I know that. You know that. Nevertheless, you need to realize that when stories are told "out of time," apart from the actual "right now" needs of the trainee, they are likely to be forgotten and not available when needed. This is why so much attention must be paid to telling stories so well that they will be remembered in any case just because they were so cool.

Recognize That Story Living Is Better Than Story Telling

Listening is something people do all the time, but they still don't do it all that well. Mostly they remember their own experiences. (*What happened in that conversation you had with Joe? Well first I told him, and then I said, and I really zinged him with this one.*)

People don't do so well at remembering what the other guy said or did. What they do remember is their own experiences. (Of course, what they remember of their own experiences is the stories they told about those experiences.)

So while it is important to hear stories, it is more important to tell them. And while it is important to tell stories, it is more important to live them (which helps in having them to tell of course).

> *Story living means having meaningful experiences.*

Story living means having meaningful experiences. In training this means allowing people to actually do something rather than hear about what others did. It means having every experience be complex and realistic as opposed to short and superficial. It means that, instead of teaching the principles of something, you let people practice the details over and over again. You can't learn to hit a home run from a training video.

Surprise Your Listener

Stories that are remembered are those that are surprising in some way. The story of Billy is surprising for two reasons. First, the "Don't die, Billy!" cheer is one that you don't expect on a ball field. Second, you don't expect a baseball player who's hit a homer to stop at third for health reasons. Those surprises are what make it a good story.

When you tell stories, make sure they contain at least two surprising elements. When stories fail to surprise at all, they cannot be remembered at all. They simply match what is already in your head and meld together with everything else you know.

> *When stories fail to surprise at all, they cannot be remembered at all.*

And of course, what is surprising to one person may not be surprising to another listener. Surprise is, after all, a relative concept. Not everyone is surprised by the same stuff. After enough "don't die" stories, I would fail to find this story of interest. The second one would help confirm the first one, making it a pattern that I might expect to see again and again. But after that, my interest would flag.

Audiences are full of different people who understand and relate to and are surprised by different stories. Good storytellers understand this and choose stories that work for their listeners as well as they can.

Remember Billy

Remember that Billy chose the story to tell as he was creating it. He not only lived his story, he decided which story to live. He thought about telling a story as he made the choice of what story he would tell. He may not have explicitly thought this of course, but that is what happened.

Select wisely the stories your company chooses to live and then tell. Be involved in the story selection process, not only the storytelling process. The spinmeisters of politics spend much time trying to tell a story that is different from the story that was actually selected by their bosses. Being part of the story selection team, making choices as the company conducts its business, helps a trainer have good stories to tell.

Some weeks after Billy's triple, I hit a home run. This is such an infrequent event that I could simply not remember the last time I had hit one. I thought about Billy as I was rounding third. My heart isn't in such good shape either.

Billy was there to greet me at the plate. He was wondering why I hadn't stopped at third. Me too. Guess I couldn't wait to tell the story.

◊   ◊   ◊

JUMP START YOUR TRAINING

THINGS TO THINK ABOUT WHEN HEARING A STORY
- What would the opposite story be? Could the person who is telling the story have told the opposite story? Or

is he simply telling a story that everyone expects him to tell?

- Why does the teller think you will care about her story? Is she simply trying to be funny? Does she have a point? What is the point? Is the point surprising?

- Why do people tell stories? Do they want to impress? Do they want you to empathize? Are they trying to make themselves heroes? Do they want your admiration?

- Why do we live a story? Why do people behave as if they were in a story that someone else wrote? Can people create their own life stories or is this too hard or too radical?

- Is the story we are hearing new in any way? Or is it simply a retelling of an old story? If it is new, in what way is it new? What can be learned from the story?

Things to Think About When Telling a Story

- Why does anyone want to hear this story? Could I publish this story or is it for only certain people's ears?

- How does the story make me look? Is this the way I want to be seen?

- What can my listeners take away from my story? Do they already know what I am trying to tell them? Am I insulting them by being obvious? Am I boring them by being repetitive?

- Is this story germane to the context? Does this story work in certain situations and not in others? Why does it work in one place and not another?

- Do I know who my listeners are? Are they capable of hearing my story? Do they need preparation in order to understand my story? Will they learn anything from my story? Do they care about what I am saying?

10

What's Doing?

THE EXCUSES FOR NOT DOING DOING-BASED TRAINING—
AND HOW TO AVOID THEM

Community colleges suffer from an awful reputation that leaves them all with an inferiority complex. Not so long ago I heard a comedian say that if you ask a student at one of the well-known universities where she goes to school, she simply tells you. But if you ask a community college student, he gives all kinds of excuses about credits and money and why he happens to be going to a community college he is not proud to name.

This is all rather ironic since it has always seemed to me that of all the kinds of schools there are, community colleges are some of the least broken. If an adult wants to learn photography, he can sign up for a community college course that will have him taking pictures, making prints, and so on until he gets good at it. These courses are market-driven, so they need to provide what students want rather than what professors feel like providing, as is the case in four-year colleges.

So I was rather surprised when a community college asked me to give them advice. I toured their classes and, since I love to eat, was most curious about their cooking classes meant to train chefs. I walked into the classroom expecting to see a lot of seats and a lectern and instead found twenty stoves with full paraphernalia. "You don't need my help," I declared, "if students are cooking and you are helping them do it better, you are doing all that needs to be done."

It is a simple enough truth. We learn by doing. This is an idea as old as Plato. But somehow schools keep screwing this simple idea up. Now it is not my point here to talk about school, so the question is, how does corporate training, which is presumably about getting people to do their jobs better, somehow manage to fail to put the equivalent of a fully equipped kitchen in front of every trainee?

A SIMPLE TRUTH

We learn by doing.

How do they fail to teach doing?

Let me count the ways.

THE TOP TEN REASONS WHY CORPORATE TRAINERS FAIL TO TEACH BY DOING

#10 Real-life situation is too hard to replicate in a classroom

#9 It takes too long to have trainees actually try things out

#8 There are no experts available for the one-on-one help that is required in a practice situation

#7 They want to teach general principles and you can't easily do that by doing

#6 It is hard to do things on the web

#5 The equivalent of a fully equipped kitchen is sometimes very expensive to recreate

#4 The subject matter doesn't seem doing oriented

#3 The training department has a list of learning objectives that can be learned without doing

#2 There is a corporate knowledge base that has to be learned, and this has nothing to do with doing

And the top reason is

#1 They don't know how to do it

It makes sense to start with number 1.

Why Don't Corporate Trainers Know How to Teach by Doing?

One answer is that since nearly everybody has attended schools in which learning by doing is a rarity, it would be surprising to discover that those who build training have suddenly revised the methodologies by which they themselves were trained.

Since eating is on my mind (perhaps I am hungry as I write this), I am reminded of a meal I had some years ago. I have a French friend who is a food fanatic. (You might think that all French people are food fanatics, but it really isn't true.) At the time of this story my friend lived in Paris. He heard that I was in Brussels at the moment, so he called and said he was coming up and then we would go to eat in Germany. Now Germany isn't exactly a hop, skip, and a jump from Brussels, and there are plenty of good restaurants in Paris as well as Brussels, so it seemed a long way to go for a meal.

But my friend did indeed fly into Brussels, and we did indeed have a superb meal that night in Brussels, but the next day, there was my friend with a rented car and a reservation in Groivenbroich, Germany. Now Groivenbroich, needless to say, is not exactly on the beaten track. It is near Dusseldorf, but it is not at all clear that even the people in Dusseldorf have discovered it yet. Anyway my friend had, probably because Michelin gave them two stars and the French live by the Michelin Guide when they are outside of France.

Nevertheless I was prepared for the worst. I am a food nut after all, and Germany is not exactly the center of the food universe.

We arrived in what looked like any other German town and entered what looked like any other German hotel in a small German town. The dining room was undistinguished and there were waitresses instead of waiters, an occurrence that lets you know that you are outside of France for sure. Suddenly, I was excited. I knew I was in for a special treat.

To understand why I was excited, you would have to understand something about the Michelin Guides.

The Michelin raters are hooked on ambiance. The people who rate the restaurants are not wealthy, they work for a publication and are paid accordingly. The raters don't eat so well every day, so when they are doing their rating, they want the works. They want people slobbering over them. Giving two stars to a dull place without class (according to French standards that is)? The food would have had to be awfully good.

And a feast it was. The only real problem was the menu which, since it was written in German of course, seemed to call every dish *fleischwafen* or something like that, which in addition to being unpronounceable also seemed very unappetizing. It all sounded like German food to me. But it wasn't. In fact, it wasn't any particular type of cuisine at all. It was, simply . . . original.

So How Do You Learn to Be Original?

Somewhere in the middle of the meal we called over the chef and asked him where he had learned to cook.

"Which great French chef have you trained with?" we asked.

"I haven't really trained with anybody," he said.

In fact, he hadn't even been able to get a reservation at the best restaurant in Paris the last time he was there and he was hoping that maybe we could help him next time he was in Paris?

So what does this have to do with your training situation?

Every dish at Zur Traube was inventive, novel, different, not like you'd ever had before.

Why?

Because the man didn't have anyone to teach him. No one had let him wash their dishes or chop celery while he had the creativity knocked out of him. He couldn't learn to copy Paul Bocuse's style, or George Blanc's pancakes. He had had to invent it all himself. Few of us are so lucky. Most of us get training. Some of us get training from the best. Herr Kaufman had to figure it out on his own. *He learned by doing.*

One problem with this story is that it may sound a bit like I am advocating something like letting a million monkeys type on a computer hoping that one of them will write a great novel. If no one ever gets trained, then only luck produces a great master. And, no, I wouldn't recommend that corporations let everyone figure it out on their own for twenty years, hoping that some employee invents some new stuff.

But I also don't recommend that each employee be given training that tells him or her what the truth is.

Without training, Herr Kaufman had to figure out more than a few things for himself. It is possible to be creative by reasoning from prior cases, but it is also possible to be even more creative if you have no prior cases. It is just also a whole lot more risky. Herr Kaufman took a chance with each dish he created.

And he succeeded wildly. He is an original, and even the established raters had to recognize that.

But of course, not every corporation wants or needs originals. They simply want people who know how to do their jobs, so my story isn't really relevant, right?

Well, maybe it is . . .

He had no training, but Herr Kaufman had access to a stove. He ran a kitchen at some point. He demonstrated enough skill to be able to open a business. He just didn't have instruction. How important is instruction really, when all is said and done? In Herr Kaufman's case, not very.

What is important then? Practice. Practice is what matters. Herr Kaufman had a restaurant to practice in. *Feedback.* Feedback is also important. He had customers, reviewers, raters, all kinds of people who could tell him what they thought. And one more thing. *Reflection.* He had time to think about what went wrong and what went right. He could try try again.

And perhaps most importantly, he had no one trying to bother him with the general principles behind the theory of cooking, which might have made him a scholar on the history of gastronomy but would have been unlikely to improve his cooking skills at all. Good baseball hitters don't usually expound on the physics of the curve ball. They just hit it.

Elements of Herr Kaufman's Doing-Based Education

- Practice
- Feedback
- Reflection

And no one trying to teach him theory, principles, and such that have nothing to do with cooking skills.

Even if you don't want to make creative originals, and all you want is to train competent performers, these three elements are still on the critical path: *Practice, Feedback, and Reflection.* These are the elements of a doing-based education. The instruction is the least important.

So, number 1 on my list above is simplified. You don't know how to use a doing-based method? Translate doing into the three elements of practice, feedback, and reflection.

Nine More Excuses for Not Doing Doing-Based Training (and How You Can Do It Anyway)

To see how this works let's consider the other nine reasons why doing is hard. Let's start with the easy ones.

The Subject Matter Doesn't Seem Doing Oriented

Of course this is the most common problem in creating doing-based training. It is in many ways the simplest to deal with. The usual observation is that some things simply cannot be taught that way. My response is that I have never met a subject who could not be taught using learning by doing.

Once, in a passion to prove this to people once and for all, we built some software to teach art history. Now there is a dull subject. My image of an art history class is a large darkened lecture hall with a professor droning on about a slide he is showing the class and half the students asleep. Maybe this isn't always the case, but when the lights are out the students tend to nod off. Less of a doing-based subject there wouldn't appear to be.

In our program students played the role of an investigator of art fraud who had to examine several well-known pieces of art whose authorship was in dispute. They were guided by the professors, saying the same things he might have said in class about the distinctive features of an artist's work, but this time students were listening with an eye toward what they were going to do with that information. The professor was not giving a lecture but only bits and pieces of knowledge as needed. And the students were having fun. A large improvement over the learn by listening method.

Believe me, if you can do this for art history you can do this for any subject. Everything involves some doing after all. If something has no doing in it, then what is the point of learning it? Just to know it? Inert knowledge, stuff that is never used, is easily forgotten.

The Real-Life Situation Is Too Hard to Replicate in a Classroom

The art history course was a computer simulation after all. Not everyone can build such simulations. Sometimes a classroom is all they have. Could you do an art fraud investigation without a computer program?

Well, of course you could.

You would need an expert on hand, of course. He would make suggestions, but not tell. He would pose problems and then allow students to work together to figure out solutions. He would provide hints of where answers could be found. He would respond to conclusions drawn by the students by checking to see whether they could draw those conclusions from the evidence they had so far examined. In other words, he would teach Socratically. And as long as he behaved in this way, not as a fountain of information but as a proposer of problems, a pointer to information, and as an evaluator of solutions, the students would have an effective and interesting experience in which they would learn by doing. Socratic teaching and learning by doing are intimately connected.

So why doesn't everyone teach this way? Actually the answer is simple. It takes too long.

"Lectures are a very efficient way of delivering information."

This is a quote from a faculty member I know who shall remain nameless. Teachers love to believe this because it makes their lives easier. Just talk and then it's the student's problem to understand what the heck you were saying. And, I might suggest, you should talk as fast as you can because the faster you talk the more efficient you are at delivering information.

It Takes Too Long to Have Trainees
Actually Try Things Out

In fact, this one is right. It does indeed take more time to teach Socratically, and learning by doing will take longer than learning by listening every time.

The real issue is retention, not time spent in class. What will they remember of an hour spent sitting and listening versus an hour spent doing? There will indeed be more material covered in the first hour, but if less is retained, what does it matter?

Time is the enemy of education.

Who said that?

Me.

This time issue rears its head again and again in discussion of training and education. The odd thing about this issue in education is: you have thirteen years (in K-12), isn't that enough time? The reason it isn't enough time to do things right is that standards exist that are so complex, so entrenched, and so political that there is hardly time to breathe for the typical teacher in a typical classroom.

> *Time constraints are the enemy of learning by doing. It takes time to practice—and without practice there is no real learning.*

This very sad state of affairs keeps schools from using learning by doing, but it shouldn't be an issue in training. What is an issue is that somehow the people who pay for training ordain that there should be a one-hour training course in X, as if you can learn anything at all in an hour.

Time constraints are the enemy of learning by doing. It takes time to practice. But without practice there is no real learning. Tell that to your CFO.

Don't let time ruin your training course. Teach what can be reasonably learned in the time available. That will always be less than you think if the time includes time for practice, feedback, and reflection.

There Are No Experts Available for the One-on-One Help That Is Required in a Practice Situation

This can be a real issue. When the expert in quality assurance is not available, for example, and you try to train people in it anyhow, you are trying something that really is unrealistic. Replacing the expert by the textbook has never really worked in school, so I don't know why it should work in training.

But if this really is your problem, there is a solution. You must interview the experts, get all their stories on videotape, and then index the stories to problematic situations in the scenarios you create for students to use in order to learn by doing. Databases of this sort are significant not only because they are useful for learning by doing but also because they serve as an archive of information that can be used by your company.

Getting your experts on tape matters. But, *hours of videotape are useless unless they have been indexed to questions that the stories you collect answer.* Don't simply record a three-hour interview. Make sure every expert tells her stories one after the other with no story lasting more than a minute or two. Then, with hundreds of stories collected in this fashion, figure out what questions the stories answer and make these questions and answers available to your employees.

And now we come to . . .

THE HEART OF THE PROBLEM

There Is a Corporate Knowledge Base That Has to Be Learned and This Has Nothing to Do with Doing

That one, of course, and this one:

The Training Department Has a List of Learning Objectives That Can Be Learned Without Doing

Learning objectives is a phrase that literally makes my stomach turn when I hear it. Learning objectives always seem like a good idea at the time of curriculum design. Instructional design courses teach you how to make lists of them, apparently since lists are easy to find in every course design. "At the end of the course the student will know X." Sounds good.

One problem of course is that in school, when you decide that students who take a given course should come out knowing X, it is very tempting to test to see if they do in fact know X. To make sure they know it, the teacher tells X to them a lot, makes them read about X, gives them short quizzes about X, and finally examines them to see if, in fact, they know X.

Here is a learning objective I found in a fifth-grade social studies curriculum:

Student will be able to identify effective communication skills

You know and I know that this means there will be a test. But what will the test be on? Well, it would pretty well have to be on the list of effective communication skills that were given to the student. So you see the problem here. It isn't that there will be a test to see if the student knows how to communicate. It is that the curriculum now has to have in it some explicit statement of communication that may not be so important to learn, but is easy to test. Do we in fact learn to communicate by being able to identify a set of rules about effective communication?

I don't think so.

I doubt that teachers who have to teach this think so either. Communication involves actually communicating, not saying stuff about communicating.

Here is another learning objective from the same list:

> *Student will be able to identify constructive elements in a relationship and destructive elements in a relationship.*

Bear in mind that this is a fifth-grade social studies curriculum and not a graduate psychology course. It is that word "identify" again. If what we want is for students to be able to get along with one another, then they have to try new behaviors out. It is easy to say the words about being helpful to someone else. *Being* helpful is harder. Learning objectives tend to trivialize complex issues by making them into sound bites that can be told and then tested to see whether you were listening.

Learning objectives tend to trivialize complex issues by making them into sound bites that can be told and then tested to see whether you were listening.

Another problem is that when course designers get together to write a list of learning objectives, the lists go on and on. See, once you let someone start writing a list of learning objectives, two things happen every time. First, the list keeps getting longer and longer because someone realizes something "important" was left out. Second, the list tends not to relate to anything anyone will ever actually be able to do in this world.

Do not make lists of learning objectives for training courses. There is no reason to copy what schools are not doing well. If you must have a list of objectives, make them performance objectives, a list of things you want trainees to be able to do. Then make sure that any trained employee can, in fact, do them.

Okay. So if now you agree that you want to try teaching using learning by doing, you still have . . .

A Couple of Remaining Problems

It Is Hard to Do Things on the Web

And . . .

The Equivalent of a Fully Equipped Kitchen Is Sometimes Very Expensive to Recreate

These are real issues. They do have solutions, however. The key to both is to put your training on the web and then make sure that it is project-driven. Instead of thinking of training as stuff to be transmitted by your organization, you need to think of training somewhat differently.

Try Approaching Training as Learning by Doing

Think of a project that people in your organization do or a scenario that they encounter. Then recreate that project or scenario in text. Explain the conditions of the situation and the work that needs to be done. Establish clear deliverables and deadlines. Then, you need to do the following:

1. Set up teams to work together.
2. Set up mentors to help the teams when they have questions.

3. Set up simpler projects and deliverables or break the main deliverable into smaller chunks as a way to make a complex project tractable.

4. Create information online that will help them get started, offering hints and texts that will help.

5. Point to textual material that will guide them (a book on how to do it, company mentors, and such).

6. Teach mentors to teach Socratically. They should not provide answers—only suggestions.

7. Make sure the deliverables are evaluated by experts and that they give good feedback.

All of this can (and should) be online. Teams can meet online. Mentors should mentor online (allowing the best and brightest to mentor asynchronously). Deliverables should be delivered online and evaluations received online.

Doing all this allows experts to be available. It also enables learn by doing to be done on the web without building elaborate simulations. The whole scenario and team interactions and deliverables is the simulation, in effect. Of course this won't work where you need the equivalent of a kitchen, but it works very well when written materials, software, presentations, and such are the ultimate deliverable.

A Sample Scenario

At CMU West, we have been using these kinds of learning-by-doing project-based scenarios as the basis of master's degree programs. These master's programs consist entirely of projects; there are no classes to attend. To get an idea what these online scenarios look like, here is the beginning of one from our e-Business MSIT:

From: Len Walsh
Subject: eCommerce initiative benefits to Moffett
Hi,
In our last meeting with the CEO, Dara Griffith, we discussed the strategic benefits the planned eCommerce initiative would bring to the organization.
Following that meeting there was more discussion on the subject and the Moffett board has decided that our task force should carry out an in-depth analysis before an investment in eCommerce can be committed. The report on this analysis should propose specific eCommerce initiatives and the related benefits to Moffett Foods. So here's what we need you to do:

Produce a report that justifies going ahead with an eCommerce initiative at Moffett Foods. (You may consider a null solution acceptable if it leads to the best outcome.) Provide answers to the following questions/statements as part of your analysis and recommendation:

1. Identify the inefficiencies in the existing distribution system and supply chain of Moffett Foods that the eCommerce initiative will address.
2. Design a solution to enable online purchasing of Moffett Foods' products by retailers. What business benefits would your solution provide Moffett and its retailers?

3. Design a solution to enable online purchase of inputs by Moffett from various suppliers. Which specific inputs (for example, raw materials or packaging material) are suitable to be part of this system? What advantages would accrue to Moffett and to suppliers if they participate in this initiative?

The following aspects need to be evaluated and elaborated on in the solution:

- Will the eCommerce activity generate only cost savings, or will it generate additional revenues?

- Will revenues come from enhanced market reach, from new market segments hitherto untapped, or from both?

- What are the cost implications of setting up this eCommerce initiative? Is it justified to make an investment in this initiative?

- Will it provide Moffett a competitive advantage? Will the advantage be short-term or long-term? What are the possible ways of creating long-term competitive advantages, if any?

- What will be the impact on the organization's processes? Will they change drastically? If so, will a change-management effort be required?

- How technology-proficient are the suppliers and immediate customers (retailers) of Moffett? Will a change-management effort be required at suppliers' and retailers' ends to get them to participate in Moffett Food's eCommerce initiative? Will Moffett have to make an investment on behalf of players in the supply chain?

Identify and elaborate on the strategic, financial, technical and implementation risks of the proposed eCommerce initiative.

Please use the attached template for preparing this report.

Thanks and good luck!

Len Walsh, VP, eCommerce Initiatives

To help the student proceed, there are various guides and pointers to readings. Here is one such guide:

SAMPLE STEP-BY-STEP GUIDE

1. Review the analysis objectives and evaluation requirements listed in Len Walsh's e-mail.

2. Download the template for the analysis and recommendation report and read carefully through it, as it details the scope and required depth for the analysis.

3. Download and read through the case material on Moffett Foods for the background information necessary to carry out the analysis.

4. Read through the reading and external resources, including faculty video lecture for guiding concepts and information that will be helpful for your analysis.

5. Submit the analysis and recommendation report to your mentor for review. Begin reading for the next task.

6. Please note that there is no correct answer for any given problem. The scope of solution throughout this task is flexible and can be justified by giving sound assumptions and reasoning. The case material provides required information for analysis, but the information available may not be exact in some cases and may be lacking in others. It is recommended that you state the assumptions you make for lack of data in case materials. Secondary research can also supplement lack of data.

For instance, cost implications for eCommerce initiatives needs to be evaluated as part of the analysis. Information regarding this is not available in the case. The expectation is not to provide an exact cost estimate, but a range within 10 percent of the appropriate answer. A rough estimate on cost can be obtained by doing secondary research.

8. When your mentor returns your work with feedback, revise the document and resubmit it for approval.

9. Continue work on the next task.

You can build this sort of thing in your organization as well. It just takes thinking about training as learning by doing—plus time, money, patience, and the will to do it.

And now we move to . . .

The Last Excuse for Not Doing Doing-Based Learning

They Want to Teach General Principles and You Can't Easily Do That by Doing

Right.

I have often thought that principles are the last refuge of scoundrels.

◊   ◊   ◊

JUMP START YOUR THINKING

Learning by doing is not a new idea. Some wisdom from the ages to jog your consideration:

Men are born ignorant, not stupid; they are made stupid by education.
BERTRAND RUSSELL

Nothing in education is so astonishing as the amount of ignorance it accumulates in the form of facts.
HENRY ADAMS

The best way to come to truth being to examine things as really they are, and not to conclude they are, as we fancy of ourselves, or have been taught by others to imagine.
John Locke, *An Essay Concerning Human Understanding*

True information is mainly derived from experience
ALEXIS TOCQUEVILLE

That all our knowledge begins with experience there can be no doubt . . . no knowledge of ours is antecedent to experience, but begins with it.
IMMANUEL KANT, *The Critique of Pure Reason*

According to my view, any one who would be good at anything must practice that thing from his youth upwards, both in sport and earnest, in its several branches: for example, he who is to be a good builder, should play at building children's houses; he who is to be a good husbandman, at tilling the ground; and those who have the care of their education should provide them when young with mimic tools.
They should learn beforehand the knowledge which they will afterwards require for their art. For example, the future carpenter should learn to measure or apply the line in play; and the future

warrior should learn riding, or some other exercise, for amusement, and the teacher should endeavor to direct the children's inclinations and pleasures, by the help of amusements, to their final aim in life.
PLATO

As we know not anything among individual things which is more excellent than a man led by reason, no man can better display the power of his skill and disposition, than in so training men, that they come at last to live under the dominion of their own reason.
BARUCH SPINOZA

Education is an admirable thing, but it is well to remember from time to time that nothing that is worth knowing can be taught.
OSCAR WILDE

11

Pardon Me, I Must Have Misplaced My Stereotype

THE PROS AND CONS OF STEREOTYPING—
AND HOW TO TEACH PEOPLE TO DO IT WELL

I don't only play softball. I also play racquetball.

The people I play with are also old. I live in Florida, where everyone is old.

One curious thing that takes place in situations like this is something I have come to call the racquetball theory of life. People show up and play. Everyone has a first name, but no one has a last name—kind of like Alcoholics Anonymous. After a game people rest and they talk for a while. No one really knows who anyone is. They don't know if they are married, or have children or what they did for a living (most are retired). All that matters is how well you play racquetball. I think there is a life lesson there, but that is not the point of my story.

One guy who plays regularly loves to say right-wing political things and this usually causes arguments (or violent agreement). As for me, I just make wacko remarks. I don't really enjoy getting into the kind of debate that tends to leave reason or actual established facts out of the argument, which is typical of the conversations that take place between racquetball games at this gym. When things get out of hand, I am inclined to make the pithy oddball remark, just because I lose patience. I don't come off as the reasonable intellectual by doing this, as you might imagine.

I am telling you this to set the stage for one particular conversation.

Someone asked me if I had seen the movie *A Beautiful Mind*. I responded that I had, and that I had liked it. And then I added, "It was an odd movie but it was about the academic world and I suppose I resonated to that because I am an academic."

This provoked a response from someone who I know to have been a hot shot lawyer in his time. (He still goes North in the summer to work with his old firm.) He said, very haughtily, "What kind of academic are you?"

I was rather surprised at the tone he took, but I realized that he considered himself the intellectual in the crowd. He certainly didn't see me as being any kind of scholar, and I don't blame him. I don't particularly act the part on the racquetball court.

I told him that I was a professor and he responded with "Where?" said in way that made it clear he didn't think being a professor at Palm Beach Atlantic University would count. When I mentioned where I had professed, my history included Yale, where he had gone to school, and from that point until the point that I am writing this, his entire tone has changed when he speaks to me. I went from being the guy who says weird stuff to the guy who makes him just a little nervous in an argument—all with one little word that established (in his eyes) that I was somebody.

He was stereotyping me, making assumptions about who I am and what I am capable of, based on some rather superficial interactions, both before and after I had mentioned Yale.

I get the same response when I walk into a car dealer looking to buy a new car. I don't dress particularly well on those occasions and so, unless they have seen the car in which I have arrived, I am usually treated as someone who could not possibly be a serious buyer of this very important car that they have to sell.

My daughter got the same treatment when she tried to buy a wedding dress without having brought her mother along. Apparently serious wedding dress buyers always bring their mothers. But my daughter is quite grown up, her parents are divorced, she doesn't live near either my ex-wife or me.

None of this matters in the wonderful world of stereotypes.

People who interact with the public in the course of their business lives tend to rely on stereotypes. They make assumptions about the people who enter into their world and quickly judge whether they are likely buyers or whether they are troublemakers or whether they are honest and so on. They do this all the time. They decide who you are and deal with you accordingly. Of course this is bad and we should develop training to fix it.

> *People who interact with the public in the course of their business lives tend to rely on stereotypes.*

But Is Stereotyping Really Bad?
And Can Training Fix It?

Most people assume that stereotyping is bad. Certainly the word has a bad reputation. We are supposed to give everyone an equal chance, to see who they are based on what they do and say and not on what they look like or appear to be. But this is harder than it seems. To see why let's look at a fairly random news story:

Mexican Troops Kill 3 in Border Shootout

By REUTERS

"MONTERREY, Mexico, Aug. 1—Mexican troops fired a rocket-propelled grenade at a car convoy of drug trafficking suspects early this morning, killing three people and wounding six others in the border city of Nuevo Laredo.

"The shootout, in the upscale Longoria district in downtown Nuevo Laredo, started at 2 a.m. after the city police tried to stop a convoy of vehicles believed to be owned by a drug trafficking gang responsible for the killing of two police officers in a restaurant this week.

"Officials said the convoy's passengers opened fire when ordered to stop, and army troops and federal police officers were called in.

"Francisco Tomás Cayuela, the attorney general of Tamaulipas State, said soldiers fired rocket-propelled grenades because the traffickers were heavily armed. 'The forces of public order have to respond with the same level of equipment that these criminals have,' he said.

"He said the assault on factions of the Gulf Cartel drug trafficking organization could signal an end to nearly seven months of violence in the city, during which the

municipal police have been the targets of kidnappings and killings."

Now answer the following questions:

1. What were the Mexican troops wearing?
2. What were the gang members wearing?
3. What types of vehicles were the gang members riding in?
4. Where were the Mexican troops when they fired the grenade?

Americans tend to stereotype Mexicans so there is a common mental image that involves having the Mexican soldiers dressed like Pancho Villa with bullets wrapped around their chests, wearing sombreros. Even after you abandon the initial desire to use this image when hearing the story and settle on an image that has the soldiers looking just like Americans (only maybe shorter and darker), you are still stereotyping. Who says soldiers wear green camouflage outfits in Mexico? Do you really know what they wear? Are Mexican soldiers really shorter and darker on average than American troops? Probably, but who knows?

The fact is that the truth doesn't matter much here. We go with images we have. Now some of those may be seen as bad stereotypes, but some of these are actually really important stereotypes. You can't have the Mexican soldiers running around naked in your imagination. They have to be wearing something. So you mentally dress them in some outfit that is a stereotype. It is important to do so. When we imagine, we have to imagine details too, even if we don't dwell on them. You must make assumptions or the final picture you paint for yourself is dull and blurry.

Now try this with the gang members. Were they wearing bandanas and gold chains? Or were they riding in Mercedes and dressed in black suits? That's what gang members and criminals wear in the popular imagination. We do this sort of imaging all the time if we think about what we are reading.

My last question about where the troops were located at the time is meant to really bring the reality of this problem to mind. Did they fire from behind foliage? Were they on top of a hill? Did they trap them in a drive by? My favorite image has them facing off on the main street as I hum "The Streets of Laredo."

You have to do this sort of thing in order to comprehend anything. We must embellish impoverished images. If we don't then we wind up asking the speaker seemingly irrelevant questions—like "What were the soldiers wearing?"—and looking like idiots. So we simply make assumptions. And what happens when you make assumptions is that you find that you are quite often wrong. People note this when they see a movie based on a book they have read. They imagined the characters or the setting differently, and often they liked their own images better. We don't really care whether we were wrong or right when we make such assumptions. And we may or may not care if the movie makers saw the characters differently than we did.

> We have to make some sort of assumptions using information available to the mind's eye in order to comprehend anything. We must embellish impoverished images. But stereotypes also mislead, and that can be a problem.

The point is, we indeed "see" the characters in our minds. And "seeing" means stereotyping in some way—making assumptions about things you weren't told using the information available to your mind's eye. This means using stuff you already know about other people and places that you deem to be similar to the ones under discussion.

All these images are stereotypes. We rely on stereotyping in nearly everything we read, hear, and see. Stereotypes fill in the blanks. They supply the details. They make simple descriptions elegant. But they also mislead, and that can be a problem.

> *We rely on stereotyping in nearly everything we read, hear, and see. Stereotypes fill in the blanks.*

By this I do not mean that they mislead in the politically correct way we always hear about. They do that too, of course, but I am not on a social mission here. They mislead because they cause us to make mistakes, like the ones I cited above. And in business such mistakes can be costly.

So the problem, simply stated, is this:

How Do We Teach People in Business Not to Make Stereotypes

. . . when stereotypes are so darn useful in daily life (and sometimes in business too)?

The answer to this has everything to do with movies like *Pretty Woman*. We can be well-assured that those (fictional) salespeople in that Beverly Hills store who told Julia Roberts that her money was no good—and lived to regret it—would never make that mistake again. A catastrophic loss will surely convince someone to make different assumptions next time.

This is certainly learning by doing, but it is learning by doing of a frightening sort. We can't allow employees to make grievous errors in order to learn.

The Answer?

Now normally I would say simulation is the answer here. Simulations are great ways to allow people to make errors and not cause any harm to anyone while doing so. But these days high-quality simulations are deemed by most folks to be too expensive. What else can we do?

This is one of those places where stories will buy you a great deal.

So let's start with a story.

As I was writing this, *The New York Times* ran the following story:

$916.50 LATER, CABBY FINDS HE WAS
TAKEN FOR A RIDE

By DAISY HERNÁNDEZ

"It was a gamble. Alaaedien Abdelgwad, who drives a taxi, knew that much. But he also believed in good fortune and took the risk.

"At 4 a.m. on Wednesday, he agreed to drive a young man from Grand Central Terminal to Wellsville in upstate New York. Mr. Abdelgwad figured out that the fare for the 285-mile trip would be $916.50. That was two weeks' pay.

"Mr. Abdelgwad had just moved into a new apartment, and he has a fiancée in Egypt whom he wants to bring to New York.

"'I said, "If I'm lucky, I'm going to get the money,"' he said. "'If I'm not lucky, I won't get the money, and you never know.'"

"After seven hours, Mr. Abdelgwad pulled into Wellsville, which is about a two-hour drive from Buffalo. The young man, Jeremy Hartman, 23, of Eureka, Illinois,

disappeared without paying after heading to his girlfriend's house. The police found him later in a nearby apartment.

"'Mr. Hartman was charged with a Class A misdemeanor and could face up to a year in prison and a $1,000 fine,' said Jeffrey Monroe, a patrolman with the Wellsville Police Department, who found Mr. Hartman.

"Mr. Abdelgwad said that when he picked up Mr. Hartman, the young man acknowledged that he did not have any money, but he insisted that his girlfriend in Wellsville would cover the cost. Mr. Hartman gave the cabdriver a state identification card to hold until he paid the fare.

"'To make money, I have to take risks,' the soft-spoken Mr. Abdelgwad said yesterday at his home in Astoria, Queens. He had been so trusting of Mr. Hartman that he even lent the young man some cash at a rest stop.

"'I gave him money for food and drink. $15,' Mr. Abdelgwad said.

"He didn't lose faith then, he said, nor when they reached Williams Avenue in Wellsville and Mr. Hartman disappeared.

"But if Mr. Abdelgwad was not alarmed, the neighbors were: they had never seen a New York City cab pull up their street.

"'This is making me nervous,' one resident recalled telling her husband. 'What is that yellow car? It's got writing on it!'

"After she figured out what it was, said the woman, who refused to give her name, she called the police, who found Mr. Hartman an hour later in the apartment of his girlfriend's friend.

"Mr. Hartman told the police that he had driven his own car to New York from Illinois to meet a woman he had met online and who lived in Wellsville. But he had gotten lost and ended up in Times Square, he said. His car had

broken down, but officials were not sure yesterday where the car was.

"Mr. Hartman's family told the police that he had been missing since Saturday.

"Mr. Abdelgwad said he drove back to Manhattan on Wednesday and went straight to work. He worked until 2 a.m. and made $60 for the shift.

"'They say that I'm foolish man,' he said. 'No. I just try to be a good man.'"

This is the kind of mistake you would like your employees to avoid making. Properly done stereotyping is what was called for. The rider was 22. He had no money. Weren't these clues enough?

The driver had to draw on a stereotype to make a decision. A more experienced cab driver would have had the stereotype available to use to make a prediction about whether he would get paid.

So you see the conundrum.

Stereotypes are bad, but you can really screw up when you don't use them.

And you can really screw up when you do.

I was talking to a woman who used to sell houses for a real estate development company. She told me that once, when she was just starting out, she spent a great deal of time with a family who had lots of kids who drove up in a truck and said they wanted to see the most expensive house in the development. Her boss criticized her for spending so much time with what he deemed to be people who could not possibly afford the big house they were looking at. In the end they didn't buy a house from her. Was her boss right?

Certainly, salespeople must stereotype in order to make the best use of their time. On the other hand, when they stereotype wrongly, they can lose important sales. We will never know how this story turned out; the boss may have been right. The boss was indeed right about the importance of figuring out who you are talking to, but we don't know if he was right in this particular case. Perhaps this family bought an expensive house someplace else, from someone else.

Stereotyping is a skill. It may seem odd to say that, but if you can figure who is a buyer you will do a lot better as a salesperson. So how can you learn the skill of stereotyping?

Certainly it is a very important skill, not only for salesmen.

One of the stories in this book is about airport security, which is an easy thing to make fun of these days. When they make a special selection of a U.S. Senator or a ninety-year-old lady who is in a wheelchair, the security people look like idiots. Of course, what they are doing is failing to do profiling and they are failing quite deliberately. Profiling is bad in multiracial and civil-liberties-loving America. I can't say I disagree. You just know that, were they allowed to profile, every nonwhite would be specially screened.

So we still have our conundrum. Should we or shouldn't we? I have the stereotype that says hijackers are Arab men in their twenties and thirties. Not a radical stance, but if those were all the folks who ever were screened how long would it take for hijackers who looked different to appear? Certainly in the early days of hijacking the perpetrators were not Arabs. Of course, they were usually young men.

So the issue is complex but important. We can't prevent stereotyping nor should we try. We simply have to teach employees to do it properly.

> *We can't prevent stereotyping nor should we try. We simply have to teach employees to do it properly.*

How We Stereotype

1. We rely on common images from memory.
2. We remember prior cases.
3. We form categories.
4. We remember exceptions.
5. We get a feeling.
6. We miss the forest for the trees.

The above are six common features of how people rely on stereotypes. Here is a brief explanation of each.

1. We Rely on Common Images from Memory

You can't stereotype without an image of someone else in mind. You can't imagine a soldier in full camouflage dress unless you have seen one. Mental images come from somewhere, typically our own experience, or television, or movies. We imagine what our eyes have seen. Stereotypes come from real images we have experienced.

2. We Remember Prior Cases

Stereotypes also come from stories we have heard and complex situations we have encountered. People are case-based reasoners. When they have had an experience with someone or something, they expect the next experience to be just like the last one. When you eat at Burger King for the first time, you expect it to be just like McDonald's. When you meet your second Russian, Italian, whatever, you expect him or her to be just like the last one you met. When a large family arrives in a truck and tries to buy a house, you remember the last large family that looked like them. When a girl wants to buy a wedding dress without her mother, you remember the last time that happened.

3. We Form Categories

You can't do any of this without categories. You can't see one Russian as like another unless you categorized them as Russian in the first place. These categories are often given to us by others—the media, friends, or whatever. Often categories are in common use (Arab, young, or male). But equally often categories are made up by an individual and not exactly given a label (large family arriving in truck). Such categories rely on smaller features (like poor or untidy) and are built up unwittingly (associating truck and large family with "poor," for example).

4. We Remember Exceptions

Exceptions are memorable. We need to know when our predications fail. Stereotypes are basically predictions about behavior. When we are wrong about our predictions, we don't necessarily abandon the stereotype. We modify it to record the exception, so that when we encounter the exceptional situation again, we cannot make the same mistake. "Once I assumed this poorly dressed person had no money and he turned out to be the richest guy in New Mexico."

5. We Get a Feeling

Sometimes we just have a feeling about a person. These feelings don't come from the ether or second sight. Typically, such feelings are really the same kind of stuff going on that I was just talking about but the process of retrieving from memory is not conscious, so no prior images or case come directly to mind. Our feeling is stereotyping without thinking, but the process is much the same.

6. We Miss the Forest for the Trees

A mistake we make when stereotyping is paying attention to the wrong features. We might see that the customer is very young and fail to notice that the diamond ring she is wearing is very large or that she is wearing designer clothing. Alternatively, we might see her clothing and miss her accent or her bad teeth. All of these things tell us something but what they tell us isn't always that clear to us. There is a lot of information available when seeing a person for the first time, and missing crucial stuff is easy to do.

This is what stereotyping looks like. Now the question is . . .

How Do We Teach People to Do Stereotyping Well?

The answers must focus around these issues:

- Where mental images come from
- Stories we have heard and complex situations we have encountered
- Categories and features

Create Rich Mental Images

If we wanted people to have mental images of soldiers, the best way to do this would be to have them interact with actual soldiers. We could have them work in a military installation and after a while they would get mental images (and therefore stereotypes) that they could rely on in their future dealings with soldiers. Assuming this was some sort of international installation, we could assume that soon enough a reasonably accurate picture of a Mexican soldier would emerge for use in understanding the story I started with.

Training, however, is about shortening the time period for learning. We could let someone work in a facility for a year, but we want our employees to learn the same material in a week or in an hour. So how do you learn to form these mental images in a shorter period of time? Bearing in mind that images come from images, movies work fine. One's images often come from movies or TV, and that works well enough. While ordinarily I don't believe in passive learning and watching, this is one area where it makes sense. Seeing various kinds of customers, live or on videotape, can help an employee learn to stereotype properly.

The problem is not how to get employees to form these images: show them memorable situations and images. The problem is to know what your theory is and to know whether your theory is reasonable.

> *The problem is not how to get employees to form images of certain kinds of customers. The problem is to know what your theory is and to know whether your theory is reasonable.*

When the real estate boss expected the agent to ignore the family in the truck, was he right?

When the wedding dress saleswoman ignored my daughter shopping without her mother, was she right?

When the cab driver took the kid without money to upstate New York, was he right?

It is easy enough to see that these decisions, while seemingly right or wrong in any given instance, could well be cumulatively right over the long haul. In fact, the saleslady who ignored my daughter is the top saleslady in that store.

Obviously, this is a company's decision. Let her continue to behave that way or not? She will sell a lot, but she will alienate a small percentage of potential buyers. Ironically, this is the very issue in stereotyping that annoys everyone. A particular ethnic group may be statistically unlikely to buy, but some of them do buy so do you ignore all of them because the chance of a sale is low. This is exactly why people are horrified by stereotypes. They make people feel bad.

Young people without money and daughters shopping without mothers will never band together and bring a lawsuit, so there are no legal questions here, simply ones of good business practice. Since my issue here is training, my point is simply this: let employees see various types of customers in video and let them hear what your experts have to say about these types.

NOTE ON STEREOTYPING WELL

Let employees see various types of customers in video and let them hear what your experts have to say about these types.

Rely on Stories to Reflect Experience

This point follows from what I was just saying. It isn't only looking at various types of customers and examining your assumptions that is important here; it is also knowing what others have to say about the situation. Collecting the stories of the salesforce, organized around cases they have dealt with, can bring together a massive amount of experience to help a new person deal with future customers. The cab driver should have spent some time with other cab drivers discussing bad fares. This is best done in a non-ad hoc experience. That is, a video database of bad fare stories should be complied that would be available to new drivers to understand what to look out for.

While I don't expect that taxi companies will actually do this, I do think it can and should be done in the real estate business, for example. Who is likely to buy what, would be a very valuable set of information. There are likely to be contradictory stories in any such database, and good salespeople would want to know them all so that they could determine for themselves what a right course of action might be in each new case.

Jump starting experience is one very good reason to do training, and video case bases of customer stories can jump start experience in a very important way. This is just a new-tech way of listening to wise elders. It is really quite important. However, it does need to be coupled with video images, as I mentioned above.

Concentrate on Categories and Features

When I was about thirty years old, I attended an international conference in Scotland. At lunch one day an Italian woman of about my own age introduced herself to me. I told her my name and she responded that I was lying. "Why would I lie about my name?" I asked her. She said that she had been reading the work of Roger Schank for almost ten years now and that he was obviously a much older man than I and why was I pretending to be him? When I showed her something with my name on it she simply decided that he had given it to me and I was pretending to be him for some reason. I never did convince her.

Her categories for professor certainly contained the feature "old." This is not a bad assumption in Italy, but in the United States there are young professors, especially in high-tech fields, and this was even more true in the Seventies. She didn't know all this. She was using the wrong stereotype.

If we meet two people with the same features who do similar things, say very tall people who stoop when they walk, then we might make an assumption that all tall people stoop when they walk. We might also find a logical explanation for this (ducking low doorways all the time for example).

While this particular generalization may not matter much, how about people who talk loudly and enthusiastically about what you are trying to sell and then don't buy. If this happened a few times, wouldn't you be inclined to distrust the next person who did this and spend less time on the sale?

Determining the Key Features on Which to Base a Generalization and Build a Stereotype Is Critical to Doing It in a Beneficial Way

How can we learn to do this?

Let's return to racquetball.

Here is a key generalization: when serving to a right-handed player: try to get the ball into the left corner on the back wall. No one teaches you this strategy typically, but any good player knows it. Obviously, the strategy rests on a stereotype about right-handed players. Knowing that right-handedness is a key feature to attend to in racquetball is part of the experience one gains by playing.

Here again, the issue is jump starting experience by not forcing a learner to figure out every stereotype she might ever need. And here again, telling is unlikely to be the best strategy for doing this.

> *In jump starting experience, telling is unlikely to be the best strategy. Features and categories for generalization require not only experience but also discussion.*

Features and categories for generalization are one of those things that require not only experience but also discussion. Sometimes, when you try to generalize on your own you get it wrong.

An example: When I was campaigning against the war in Vietnam when I was a graduate student, an older man who had obviously fought in World War II told me that every generation has its war and that I was avoiding mine. A little bit of math told me that he had entered the Army in World War II at about the age I was then. He had made a generalization, based on some pretty random stuff, that when you were twenty you went to war, so stop complaining.

Politics aside, his generalization was based on age. Had he had the opportunity to discuss his stereotype with others, they might have pointed out that many people arrive at the age of twenty and have no war to be sent off to. I don't know whether this would have changed his mind about Vietnam, but he might have had to come up with a more accurate stereotype.

Learning the relevant features to use in your generalizations and learning to make reasonable categories involves analysis of experience and does not necessarily entail having had the experience. Thus, this is a good candidate for training. It requires having experiences videotaped (acted or real) and allowing trainees to talk about what they have seen and about the generalizations that can be drawn from what they have seen.

The key is to focus on the features of the actors in the scenario that are relevant to use for stereotyping. By this I obviously do not mean skin color but things like smiles a lot, or aggressively responds with questions, or is argumentative. How these things predict buying behavior (or any other kind of behavior) is very relevant for learning how to profit from the experience of others.

To do this, you have to interview your salespeople about what they look for, gathering stories as you go. Then set up scenarios that capture key features and let employees watch them and discuss them. Getting people to think about what to look for with customers is the key issue in harnessing stereotyping to your advantage.

> *Getting people to think about what to look for with customers is the key issue in harnessing stereotyping to your advantage.*

Now about that stereotype you may have been relying upon ever since I told you about Billy and the softball team and then added in the story about the retired guys I play racquetball with. You know, the one that has everyone in Florida being really old, and the guys I am talking about all being on their last legs?

The first one is not so far off. It seems that way to me too. At least the guys who have the time to play ball are pretty old. But they are a lot better athletes than you might think. Who do you think plays ball at that age, guys who never could play in the first place? Some of these guys are pretty darn good. They just don't run much.

Just another stereotype to tweak.

◊   ◊   ◊

JUMP START YOUR TRAINING

Tools for Teaching Beneficial Stereotyping

1. STATISTICS
Make use of statistics: what are the demographics of your customers, honest suppliers, helpful consultants? Don't be afraid to find out and help your employees know what to look for. People will say there are exceptions; of course there are. Teach employees to play the demographic odds.

2. ODDS
Yes, my daughter did buy a wedding dress without her mother, but the saleslady who refused to wait on her was not the top salesperson for no reason; she plays the odds. A salesperson must worry about the optimal use of her time.

3. STORIES
Since people respond well to the stories of others, especially those of people they know, create a story database of successful people interactions. When a salesperson has a success—record it. Ask him how he sized up the prospect and how he knew she

would buy. Record failures as well. Let employees learn to stereotype by hearing the successes and failures of others at stereotyping.

4. TALKING ABOUT STEREOTYPES

Let's face it, in this country stereotypes seem like a terrible idea. Get people to talk about the stereotypes they have. Help them get over their inability to say what they feel—that a poorly dressed client is unlikely to buy, for example. Have them be specific. How do you define poorly dressed? Is it the clothing or is it really something else? How do you determine whether someone can afford something? If someone dresses very well, what stereotypes does that bring up? Are they predictive?

5. PREDICTIONS

Have employees make predictions, about everything and anything. Ask them to explain their reasoning. Have the successful predictors specify their criteria. What factors were they considering? Teach people to pay attention to features in their environment in order to make predictions.

12

Every Curriculum
Tells a Story (Don't It?)

THE PROBLEMS WITH MOST CURRICULA TODAY—
AND HOW THEY INSPIRE A DIFFERENT WAY
TO DEFINE THE TRAINING DESIGNER'S JOB

For the last few years I have been building a new kind of training for both universities and for corporations that is best explained by a simple parable.

Once upon a time there was a kingdom that was overrun with dragons. The people were terrorized by the dragons so they decided to build a new curriculum in their finest university to train young warriors in the art of dragon slaying. The university they selected had a faculty that knew many different things that would be of potential use to a dragon slayer, so the faculty met and formed a curriculum committee to establish a master's degree in Dragon Slaying. The committee drew on all the wisest faculty in the university, so it had faculty from the arts and faculty from the sciences. There were business faculty and law faculty and medical faculty. The engineering faculty was represented and so was the humanities faculty. Surely from such an erudite group, the best and the brightest could instruct those who wished to learn how to slay the dragon.

At the curriculum planning meeting everyone agreed that each faculty had something important to contribute. The business faculty was concerned that potential dragon slayers understand how to finance a dragon slaying expedition and know how to create a business plan to market the story and lessons derived from a successful voyage. The engineering faculty wanted to make sure that the student warrior would know how to read maps, build bridges where needed, and launch missiles. The humanities faculty realized that dragons could be reasoned with and proposed a course in how to speak Dragonese and how to negotiate with dragons. The legal faculty was concerned with dragon rights and potential lawsuits and suggested a course in law for the neophyte warriors. The arts faculty wanted to make sure that the public would be able to see what the dragon looked like and suggested the use of photography and drawing courses. The scientists wanted to know about the habitats and evolutionary history of the dragon and therefore proposed teaching a basic course in evolution and biology to the students in the program . The medical faculty was concerned that students might not know how to kill the dragon properly if they failed to understand how dragons were constructed.

As it happened, this university was the most prestigious one in the land. Consequently its faculty were very busy working on government-funded research projects and traveling around the world giving invited speeches as well as consulting to business. They didn't really like to teach all that much and they hated to have to develop new courses because these were a lot of work. They were willing to develop some new courses, but new courses for master's students were never a priority. They each decided to choose courses from existing curricula that would be appropriate for the novice dragon slayers. In this way students would get a broad education that would serve them well. When they finished this was the curriculum they chose:

FIRST SEMESTER

Introduction to Dragonese

Basic Legal Concepts

Introduction to Photography

Introduction to Anatomy

Strength and Materials

SECOND SEMESTER

Introduction to Dragonese II

Civil Liberties and Animal Rights

Introduction to Drawing

The Anatomy of Dragons

Projectile Physics

All agreed that this was a very good curriculum indeed but that it was difficult to cover everything needed in a one-year master's program, so it was decided to make the dragon slaying master's a two-year program. This was the second-year curriculum they agreed on:

THIRD SEMESTER

Basic Negotiation

History of Warfare

Introduction to Ethics

Evolutionary Biology

Introduction to Map Reading

FOURTH SEMESTER

Introduction to Public Policy

Basic Marketing

Basic Finance

Introduction to Computation

Logistics

The faculty was very proud of this curriculum and agreed it was well-balanced and covered everything a student would need to know. A student body of twenty was recruited and they all graduated two years later, most of them with high honors. They then went out to slay dragons.

Three of them failed to win funding for their expedition and they went into other fields. Five of the remaining formed a dragon slaying team, but they had great difficulty getting along with each other. One of the members killed another one and then the rest killed him. The other three ran away and were never heard from again.

The remaining twelve were more successful. They formed three teams of four, were well-financed, and they got along well with each other. Unfortunately, the first of those teams never could find a dragon to slay, although they did spend a lot of time looking. Eventually they formed a company that trained dragon slayers.

The second team did indeed meet the dragon. Unfortunately, this was because the dragon found them first. They tried to reason with the dragon but only one of them could remember how to speak Dragonese since it was a year after they had taken Introduction to Dragonese. However, the graduate who had been good at speaking Dragonese had been the only student to fail the negotiation course. He succeeded in annoying the dragon greatly, demanding that he not breathe fire while they negotiated. The dragon ate all four members of the team.

The third team did indeed find and do battle with the dragon. Unfortunately, they had never really tried to fight a dragon before and the dragon was much faster and its flame much hotter than any of them had anticipated. The dragon chased one of the members of the team off of a cliff and then proceeded to melt first the weapons and then the body of a second team member. The last two team members had no idea how to engage a battle between just the two of them and the dragon so they negotiated a truce. They are now doing public relations for the dragon.

The dragon slaying story is my way of poking fun at how university education works. Who else but professors would think that teaching people to slay dragons would not involve actually slaying some dragons?

Well, uh, um . . . corporations?

In one of the strangest developments I have encountered in training . . .

Corporate Training Departments Have More and More Begun to Resemble Schools

They have course catalogues and multiple-choice tests and lectures delivered at a distance and lots of classes. They even call themselves universities from time to time.

This desire to copy schools has always baffled me. There seems to be an assumption that schools understand how to teach and that everything in school should be copied by corporate training departments. Why they think this I don't know. Schools were not one day designed by experts in pedagogy. Quite the contrary. They evolved based on financial issues, demands from teachers' unions, political interests, and a whole lot of randomness.

> *It is baffling that corporate training departments seem to assume that schools understand how to teach and so they should do everything that the schools do.*

One of the key aspects of school one would not want to copy is the notion of a course. There is a real problem with the very concept of a course. Universities have suffered from this problem for years, and now corporations are imitating a system that they presumably think has been ineffective.

Why do courses exist? There have always been courses it seems, so we naturally assume that courses are a fundamental building block of any educational system. But courses don't exist because they are a natural mechanism for learning. And they were certainly not designed with students' needs or interests in mind.

Courses were designed for and by the faculty that teach them.

Two things are true in any modern first-class university:

First, professors seek light teaching loads and are rewarded with light teaching loads for any number of reasons. The best universities compete over faculty, and teaching load more than salary is a main issue in that competition.

Second, professors have specialties. They know one small field really well. They cannot teach any course in their own departments much less any course in the university. They know what they worked on when they did their Ph.D. and they care to teach only what they have been working on professionally. This means that while they may be cajoled into teaching an introductory course from time to time, most professors, especially the most important ones, stay within a very narrow range that is their own specialty.

So why are there courses? Because there couldn't be anything else. If a professor only teaches three hours a week (this is hardly unusual—I taught less) and only teaches his specialty (I never taught anything else in thirty-five years), then what else could there be but specially designed courses that don't take up a very large percentage of the week?

So naturally, a full-time student would be taking four or five of these. But what would he or she be learning? He or she would certainly not be following a coherent course of study meant to teach him to be able to do something at the end. This could not come from assembling a potpourri of random courses.

That corporations follow this same line of instruction can only be madness. Or else an inability to comprehend the lack of sense inherent in a course-based system.

IDEALLY, A CURRICULUM SHOULD HAVE A GOAL

There should be an end product in mind. At the end of a given curriculum, a student should be able to function in some world for which the student has been preparing. By and large this does not happen in a university setting because university curricula consist of sets of courses that may or may not relate to each other and are usually designed to enable the professor to not have to learn anything new or design any new way of delivering the old material. They are not meant to produce capable workers in a given area.

Universities do design curricula, of course. In common usage, a *curriculum* means a course of study. And that means that schools say which courses go with which other courses to meet the requirements of graduation. But if you have ever been to a faculty meeting you know that these curricula are about making sure that every professor gets his favorite course in the curriculum, thus protecting the interests of those who teach courses that no one wants to attend, and are definitely not about producing capable employees. Universities are proud that they don't try to produce people who can work in the real world. In fact, they are really trying to produce academics and their curricula work well enough for that. But the average student does not plan on becoming an academic, so this is an odd state of affairs at best.

> *When I decided to include the dragon parable in this book, I found I didn't have a copy (because my machine had crashed a while back) so I got it from the web at www.kurzweilai.net. Along with the version posted there, there are comments from various people. Here is one of them, posted on 01/29/2002 12:55 a.m. by jsmarr@stanford.ed*

"I like the ideas here, and I agree that the current education system can't get much worse, but one important distinction that I think should be made clear is education as job-training vs. education as enabling the next generation of academia. I'm currently an undergraduate, and something I hear a lot (and agree with) is that the purpose of my education is not just to be able to get a good job, but it's to be able to think new thoughts, and to push the envelope of what we know and how we think. SCC [story-centered curriculum] is much more what I would call 'vocational education,' which is important in business and in some colleges, but is not really the job of top universities. That's not to say that you couldn't adapt the SCC paradigm to universities (i.e., tell a story of being a professor or what-have-you), but that's a slightly different vision than what's articulated. The brilliant point of the SCC that should carry over is [that] regardless of your goals, it's clear that you don't spend much time thinking or doing things that you really do when you're living those goals. So even teaching students how to be a professor by doing would be teaching them a lot that currently you have to pick up 'on the job.'"

I was struck by this because it is so Stanford. Stanford doesn't exist to train people to get a job. This is a mantra at places like Stanford. (I was a professor there too a while back.) A Stanford education is not about workplace (or even life) preparation. They tell you this early and often, because for the most part they know that the potpourri of courses you will take at Stanford will train you to do nothing.

But corporations actually do vocational training don't they? So maybe what I call the *story-centered curriculum (SCC)* is for them. The idea behind the story-centered curriculum is . . .

A Good Curriculum Should Tell a Story

That story should be one in which the student plays one or more roles. Those roles should be roles that normally come up in such a story. The curriculum is intended to teach the student how to do something. The roles should be ones that the graduate of such a program might actually do in real life or might actually need to know about (possibly because she is likely to manage or work together with someone who performs that role).

An SCC is inherently goal-based. The goals are those that a student has for entering school or training and following this curriculum in the first place. An SCC is made up of a set of real-life types of activities that comprise the bulk of the work done by the student and a set of events that occasionally interrupt or augment those activities.

How to Build an SCC

In order to understand how to build an SCC we have to understand its components. To do this, we return to dragon slaying. What would building a good dragon slaying curriculum entail?

- The first step is to determine the career goals of the student.

- The second step is to determine the key activities that comprise the life of a person who has achieved the goal that the student aspires toward.

- The third step is to determine what key events might occur in the life of a person who has achieved such a goal.

- The fourth step is to come up with a story that all the above fit neatly within.

- The fifth step is to determine what things a person entering the curriculum would need to know that are not particularly part of the story per se.

The story would be about a particular attempt to slay a particular dragon. The student would be part of a dragon slaying team that would prepare for the big event by learning to do small parts of the overall task and by practicing on simulated versions of the task that have been simplified in critical ways. In this way, when a student attempts to slay an actual dragon for the first time, he will be part of a team of student dragon slayers advised by more experienced dragon slayers.

During the simulated expedition, obstacles would be thrown the student's way that he or she may not have anticipated. These obstacles could be overcome by good reasoning and planning with the help of a tutor, by working out a plan with the student's team that divides up the roles, by special-purpose just-in-time courses that have been prepared to help students who have encountered obstacles, or by the faculty suspending time and going back to remedy any holes in a student's knowledge. When a student finally slays the simulated dragon, he is certified a Master Dragon Slayer and is ready to encounter real dragons on his own.

A story-centered curriculum, therefore, starts with the determination of what the story will be. Then within the context of that story, designers must decide on simplified mini scenarios and subtasks. The designers must not only create the story line, but also the denouement, that moment when we know we have won.

When an integrated story has been created, it is the job of the course designers to determine a set of tasks to be accomplished and to decide how students are to be taught to do the assigned tasks. This is where the traditional notions of teaching are changed.

So far, so good. But you may be asking . . .

How Does It Work?

We first tried these ideas at Carnegie Mellon's new West Coast campus on master's programs in various areas of computer science, which opened to students in the fall of 2002. As of this writing more than one hundred students have participated in an SCC at CMU West.

At CMU West students work in groups of three or four. They are given detailed information about a fictional company they are working for, together with detailed assignments. With the help of an advisor, they establish roles to play and timetables for the completion of the various assignments. Supporting materials are made available and faculty and mentors answer questions and point students in the right direction.

The simple idea here is that it is the job of the faculty to set up a reasonable story and a set of deliverables within that story and to be available to help as needed, but it is not the job of the faculty to provide information that is readily available elsewhere. Thus, the CMU faculty need not teach how to create a financial plan since this has been written about in many places. The job of the faculty is to look at the financial plans created by the students and help them make them right.

This is an iterative process that is at the heart of real teaching utilizing one-on-one tutoring. There is no place for either classes or lectures in this curriculum.

The SCC can be presented entirely online or entirely on the ground in a traditional school setting. Or a mixture of the two can be used. The main face-to-face interactions in the "on the ground" version are between the student teams who meet as a group, the tutoring sessions with a group and a tutor, and the faculty supervision and evaluation of the group's progress. All of these can be done online. A mix of the two allows face-to-face interactions when possible and still takes advantage of the opportunities offered by having the best and brightest mentors available to do the interactions at a distance.

The SCC is about the elimination of courses in favor of curricula that enable participation in a meaningful story that the student is likely to engage in after he or she is finished.

Our results so far have been impressive. Students seem to love the experience of being in an SCC and they appreciate learning by doing rather than learning by listening. But they also agree that it is a lot more work than they have ever done in school before. Students who have grown used to having a teacher tell them what to do and then doing it are initially quite shaken by this kind of experience.

What Does It Feel Like Day-to-Day to Be in This Kind of Program?

I asked one of the students at CMU to tell me what his day looks like:

DAY IN THE LIFE AT CMU WEST

By Marc Raygoza

My typical day as a remote, part-time student at CMU West is anything but typical. The following is a depiction of a typical day attending CMU West remotely.

4:45 A.M.—5:15 A.M. DAY BEGINS

Three days per week I travel 100 miles each way to work. I take the train from South Orange County to North Los

Angeles. The travel time allows me to focus on schoolwork. This is wonderful since I have an eight-month-old baby and wife who need my undivided attention when I am home.

5:20 A.M.—7:45 A.M. TRAIN RIDE (LEARNING)

The morning train ride I spend learning more about the project deliverable. I either watch the CMU classroom lecture videos or read reference materials recommended by the CMU faculty. If I am viewing the lectures, I put on my headphones to not inconvenience anybody else on the train. My objective in the morning is to ensure that I am knowledgeable in the subject area before I begin solving the current project deliverable. On this day, I am learning UML notation. The UML is used to model our system prior coding.

12:00 P.M.—12:30 P.M. LUNCH (E-MAIL)

I check my CMU e-mail during lunch. I use this time to discuss any pressing issues with my teammates. On this day, we have a 6:00 p.m. meeting, and a fellow teammate has a few questions about tonight's agenda.

5:15 P.M.—7:35 P.M. TRAIN RIDE HOME (DOING AND WEEKLY TEAM MEETING)

On the train ride home, I work on my project deliverable before the meeting. I apply the UML notation I learned in the morning. I attend the weekly team meeting by calling our team conference call number. Our mentor dials in from San Jose, California. My other team member dials in from Detroit, Michigan. I dial in from the train somewhere between Los Angeles and Orange County. We discuss status reports, issues, and action items for the next week. Our meeting is very precise and to the point. Everybody on the call is very busy with work and the CMU MSE program. On this day, our meeting lasts a little over an hour. After the meeting, I resume working on my UML project deliverable.

8:00 P.M.—9:00 P.M. HOME
(WEEKLY ONE-ON-ONE MENTOR MEETING)
On this day, I have my weekly one-on-one call with my mentor. We discuss my key project deliverables and the reference materials I am using to complete them. We discuss possible solutions and alternatives to solving a complex problem. The call ends an hour later.

This is a different way to think about education. Students at CMU West don't go to school. They work on projects with their teammates.

To Tie All of This Back to Your Training Programs

. . . the question now is: why do your trainees go to training?

Of course, they like to get out of the office for a while. So it can be great fun to travel someplace nice and enjoy a few days off. But if your goal is to have your trainees learn to do a new kind of job or do their jobs better, then it might be a better use of everyone's time if they simply worked at the new job you would like them to do in a context that realistically simulates what their new job experience might be like.

Have a Job to Train Someone for?

ASK THE FOLLOWING QUESTIONS
- Who does this job well now?
- What small tasks comprise the larger job?

- What is a sequence of tasks that comprise a typical deliverable in this job?
- What problems occur in this job that cause mistakes to be made?
- What problems occur in this job for which people find themselves unprepared?

And then . . .

Find a Good Story That Comprises All of the Answers to the Above

Doing this is a complex task but one that can be learned. The key issue is to understand the mistakes that are typical of the job to be learned and to make sure that the circumstances that cause those mistakes all occur in the story.

Then simply make up a story that includes all the problems that normally occur in the world your story talks about. Make sure there are clear deliverables in various segments of the story and make sure that there is scaffolding that helps the trainee through the story. This scaffolding would come in the form of texts, videos, team members to consult, and mentors who provide help, as well as experts who look at the deliverables and return them with helpful comments.

The story must revolve around slaying actual dragons. By that I mean that there should be a really clear goal at the end of the story that is clearly a "doing" goal. People who finish the story should be able to do at the end what they hadn't really ever done before at the beginning.

Would you have then built a course? You can call it what you like. But bear in mind that university courses are only about one subject at a time because that is all the professor can teach. The kinds of stories I am talking about can have multiple aspects to them: math as needed in the story; writing as needed in the story; personnel issues as needed in the story; the management techniques being taught as needed in the story; and so on.

A good story has many aspects to it. As does a good education. Many scholars have noted that experience is the only real teacher. Your problem, as a designer of training, is to design experiences, not courses.

◊　　◊　　◊

Jump Start Your Thinking

To keep you thinking about how you might apply the story-centered curriculum, here are two examples from business.

Case Study 1. Project Management Training at Deloitte & Touche

My company, Socratic Arts, partnered with Deloitte & Touche to develop training to accompany the rollout of a new methodology for managing software development projects. Called "Express for Software Development (ESD)," the methodology will be used to help minimize risk, control quality, and unify the software development project process across the company. The training is designed to help project managers learn how to apply ESD on their projects and train their teams to use the new methodology. The training also helps project managers explain to clients how ESD can improve the management of software development projects.

Using the story-centered curriculum approach, Socratic Arts developed a scenario where the learner plays the role of a software development project manager on a new project, SMS (Sports Management System), which involves building an online sports registration system for (the fictitious) Wylie College. The project, which has already kicked off, must be completed before students arrive for fall semester and must function reliably. The learner's project team, company, and client are unfamiliar with ESD. There are many client stakeholders who need to have buy-in, and a lot of potential future work depends on project success.

The training consists of a sequence of tasks that highlight key phases in a project lifecycle. Learners must complete a project plan employing the new ESD methodology, prepare a requirements gathering workshop for their team, develop a master testing plan, and revise the project plan to deal with "scope creep" that threatens the project late in the game. For each task, learners submit real project deliverables to mentors for evaluation and critique.

One important benefit for Deloitte of using the SCC is that it provided very flexible delivery options. Deloitte was able to deliver the eighteen-total-hour training both in two-day face-to-face sessions and remotely over a two-week period using the same curriculum materials. Learners were also able to work either in small teams or individually if needed, depending on their location and current work assignment. Mentors, drawn from experts within the firm (U.S., Europe, Asia, South Africa), provide feedback on student work and facilitate discussion groups. Because Deloitte managers travel frequently, all training materials were packaged so that they could be downloaded to a laptop for easy off-line access. An online mentor knowledge exchange allowed mentors to share and learn from one another's experiences.

CASE STUDY 2. DEVELOPING STRATEGIC PLANNING SKILLS FOR ORACLE FRONT-LINE MANAGERS

Oracle Corporation asked Socratic Arts to assist in developing the fourth and final module in its Oracle Leaders Track curriculum for front-line managers. Socratic Arts led an intensive needs analysis process that helped Oracle zero in on the most critical training needs for its front-line managers, resulting in a refocusing of the content of the module on building strategic planning skills.

Due to the constant change in the industry and within the company, new Oracle managers often find it difficult to ensure that the goals of their team are aligned with those of their business unit. To help develop managers' skills in this area, Socratic Arts worked with Oracle subject-matter experts to develop a four-step process that managers can follow to better understand their business unit's strategic goals, align their team to those goals, and communicate effectively about these goals up, down, and laterally within the company.

The training consists of coaching learners through this four-step process. Instead of employing a fictitious scenario, this curriculum has learners developing an actual plan for their own teams, using real-world inputs from their managers and business units. Thus, in addition to building skills in the training, learners also come out of the module with a real plan for their team and a plan for communicating it to their staff.

The training takes place over a five-week period and is delivered primarily at a distance. Online conferencing technology is used to convene students for weekly discussion and reflection sessions. During the fourth week, students come together for a two-day session where they present their strategic plans, get feedback, and have an opportunity to engage with a senior executive around current and future strategic initiatives and how they may impact each manager's team.

13

And We'll Have
Fun, Fun, Fun, 'til Our
Company Takes
the e-Learning Away

WHY MOST E-LEARNING IS BORING, NOT FUN—
AND REAL-WORLD TIPS FOR MAKING IT MORE ENGAGING

In 1986 I had an interesting idea. I was working in the field of Artificial Intelligence, and had by this time in my career (maybe eighteen years at that point) decided to commercialize what I had done so far. I had a number of corporate clients for whom my company was building intelligent computer programs that were meant to do all kinds of smart things. But there were all kinds of objections to building computer programs that would replace people. Maybe they would make mistakes (as if people didn't). Maybe the public wouldn't like to deal with them. Maybe they would cause labor problems.

My idea was to stop pushing the replace people idea and propose software that would help people do their jobs better. I called them advisory systems. The idea was that they would be there to help someone do his or her job instead of doing it for him or her. So instead of speaking to a computer when you called up for customer service, you would speak to a person who was essentially asking the computer what he or she was supposed to say at every given point and then the person would say it to the customer.

In order to build this kind of advisory system, you had to build a program that was as smart as one that would replace people. If anything, it was even harder to build this type of program. But it was warmer and fuzzier—no one lost his job and people still got to talk to people.

This was the origin of my interest in training. It wasn't too much of a leap from building advisory systems to building training systems. The training programs were easier to build because we didn't have to anticipate anything a customer might say. We would decide what fictional customers would say and then coach employees into the right responses.

That was sixteen years ago, as I write this. The venture capitalists who backed the company that I ran at that time thought that training was a terrible idea and suggested I do it somewhere else. In 1989, Andersen Consulting said that if I'd help fix their training (and move to Northwestern to do it) they'd give me lots of money to build new kinds of training software. So we built the Institute for the Learning Sciences (ILS) and began to invent new training stuff on the computer.

As we arrived, literally while I was driving from New Haven to Chicago, a friend of mine in Ann Arbor showed me that it was now possible to get video onto computers, and he said that would certainly change what I could build. Indeed it could, so we began with an idea of creating video scenarios with which you could interact and video experts who would talk to you, replacing the initial advisory systems that were text all the way.

Thus began the period that I now see as the most technologically exciting time in the history of training via computer. The field of computer-based training (CBT) had bored everyone into submission by this time. Every company used it. It was dull as dust and without redeeming educational value. Just text and questions. When we rolled out our first course at Andersen, the trainees refused to take it, saying it was just more of that CBT they hated. After they were forced to take it, they loved it. It was fun and interesting.

Ah, yes—fun and interesting. I remember it well.

That was before e-learning.

I receive e-mails every week or so from someone complaining about the state of e-learning. Here is a tidbit from today's e-mail from the U.K.:

> *"We have found the e-learning environment limited and quite frankly not much fun!"*

WHY ISN'T e-LEARNING FUN?

As far as I can tell, there are two reasons for this, one historical and one ideological. The historical one is more obvious, so let's start with that.

Consider, Where Did e-Learning Come From?

In 1989 when I was starting ILS and trying to revolutionize the world of training, what was I trying to change? What was there at the time? There were three things of note:

1. Lots of classrooms
2. Lots of training manuals
3. Some CBT

I fought against all of these, as you might guess, and was doing fairly well at convincing people to abandon old ways and try something new when a terrible thing happened: the web was born.

Now most people don't think the web is a terrible thing, and frankly neither do I, but its effect on the world of training was devastating. Company after company determined that their training could be, and should be, moved to the web. This seemed to be mostly an effort to save on printing and travel costs. So training directors were ordered to make the change. Typically they weren't given any new budget with which to implement this change, so the little money they had had for innovation in training—money that was quite often being used on projects to work with me and my company—now was needed elsewhere.

Suddenly training reversed its trend away from mind-numbing text followed by questions. If all the training was going to be moved to the web, then the training that was extant would simply have to be adapted to the web—that was expensive enough—and nothing new could be done.

The computer, that doing device, the device that had been used to train pilots, tank drivers, and any other profession that had money and really understood that doing was where it was at, was now being used as a glorified textbook replication machine.

How sad.

But wait, it gets worse.

Venture capitalists, those do-gooders always out to help humanity, decided to take advantage of this rush to the web. They began to invest in companies that sold technology that helped you build what is now called e-learning. They invented learning management systems, invented learning objects, and funded the building of hundreds of courses of no educational value whatsoever but which would allow a company to suddenly become an e-learning machine, full of courses they had bought and courses they had built.

Now everyone has e-learning. No one seems to like it much. It is, after all, the same CBT that was around all along, just on the web this time with better graphics.

When this didn't satisfy anyone very much, the idea of "the blended approach" was born. This meant they could still have classrooms and still have e-learning. When neither one seems better than the other, I suppose this makes sense. It just doesn't make sense to me.

> *No one ever thought as textbooks as fun so why would what amounts to no more than a textbook online be fun? Because there is a fun character who tells you to read the next section?*

So e-learning isn't fun for the same reason that the programmed texts you used in school weren't any fun. Learning was never seen as fun. It was just so much information to be gotten across. No one ever thought of textbooks as fun, so why would what amounts to no more than a textbook online be fun? Because there is a fun character who tells you to read the next section?

But of course there is a much more important reason that e-learning is not fun:

The Ideological Reason

e-Learning is not fun because, in their heart of hearts, trainers do not believe education is supposed to be fun. Oh they believe in having funny speakers, or team-building games where people laugh, or weird buttons that say funny things to wear on your lapel before or after you have been trained, but they don't think learning is fun.

Learning as hard work is an idea that has been around for a very long time, at least as long as my parents' generation in any case, who memorized Latin declensions and endless poems and speeches because it was good for you. That generation is dying off, but for the last twenty years, almost whenever I gave a speech about how learning should be fun, some old codger would get up and disagree vehemently, saying that learning was hard work and school shouldn't be fun and that was the trouble with my (Sixties) generation: "Everything has to be fun. Harumph."

Fun is an ideological issue.

Is Learning Fun? Should Learning Be Fun? What Exactly Is Funny About It?

Well, there isn't anything funny about it, and the real issue is our definition of fun, of course. I have a rather simple one myself:

Fun is when you are so totally engaged by something that at the moment you are doing it you can't think of anywhere else you would rather be or anything else you would rather be doing.

Maybe that is a weird definition, but it is mine.

So let's test it.

Is math fun?

Math was fun for me when I was in school. (I was a math major in college.) I loved the mental challenge of it, the problem-solving part of it, the competitive aspect of it (I was faster at coming up with answers than most and there were all those test scores to beat the other kids over the head with).

Somewhere in my second year of calculus it became not fun. It was too theoretical for me. I couldn't see the point. Maybe others were better at it than me. For whatever reason, math was no longer fun.

Fun is an idiosyncratic affair.

But people aren't so different from one another really. The elements of fun are the same for everyone.

> *Fun is an idiosyncratic affair, but the elements of fun are pretty much the same for everyone. The underlying concept is* engagement. *In other words, if you are really into it, that's fun.*

Everyone likes winning, for example. Everyone likes feeling that she is particularly good at something. Everyone likes getting the right answer.

Sounds like CBT should have been loads of fun then, huh? Lots of questions and answers. Lots of opportunities to beat the other guys and be good at it.

But CBT was deadly for the most part, so maybe there are more elements that comprise fun than those that I just stated.

Is reading fun?

Nothing competitive about it. Hard to say that you are really good at it. No problems to solve. Yet a lot of people really enjoy reading. So then web-based training must be a whole lot of fun, huh? Lots of reading in it.

Something is wrong here.

Fun must be defined by something else. Clearly, the underlying concept is engagement, or more colloquially: if you are really into it, that's fun.

So What Are the Basic Elements of Engagement?

Here are a few:

Fascination

Exhilaration

Confusion

Anticipation

Curiosity

Determination

Emotional identification

Excitement

Arousal

This is enough for now. It is not my intention to give a complete list here. But what is this a list of?

Are these the elements of a good novel or a good movie, for example? Well, sure they are.

Do they apply to math?

Certainly all of them don't, but most of them could for the right person.

The trick in making e-learning fun is to remember the elements of engagement.

The trick for designing really good e-learning is to make something engaging for someone who is simply not thrilled by the subject matter in the first place. I already found all these elements in mathematics as a kid, but many others did not. To make engaging e-learning in math, one would have to get all these elements in there for those who find math to be dull as dust.

> *The trick in making e-learning fun is to remember the elements of engagement. The trick for designing really good e-learning is to make something engaging for someone who is simply not thrilled by the subject matter in the first place.*

This means that e-learning would have to be exhilarating, confusing, fascinating, and so on, in order for it to work.

This is easy to say, but how exactly do you do that?

How Do These Elements Actually Get Built Into an e-Learning System?

Let's take a look at the list again:

Fascination

Exhilaration

Confusion

Anticipation

Curiosity

Determination

Emotional identification

Excitement

Arousal

Do video games qualify as fun? For some people, video games are great fun and those people would probably say that all the above elements are present in video games. But for those who think blasting space invaders out of the TV set is not fascinating, exhilarating, or arousing, then video games are not fun. So while this definition of fun (of the type we mean) seems to be useful in defining fun, it still doesn't tell us how to do it.

So let's consider two kinds of fun that have nothing to do with learning, roller coasters and movies. Personally I hate roller coasters. When I took my then-eight-year-old son on Space Mountain (an indoors and dark roller coaster at Disney World) he asked, after I released the crush-hold I had on his chest that was intended to keep him from falling out: "What was the point?"

Indeed.

Nevertheless, we can say the following. Those who like roller coasters find them fascinating, exhilarating, and just a little bit confusing. They are excited by the anticipation of each hill and aroused by the descent. They are determined to not get sick and to make it to the end intact. They emotionally identify with those who don't make it and are basically curious about why the whole thing works.

Not I. I experience none of that. A good movie, on the other hand, one where I identify with the characters and anticipate what is going to happen next and am aroused, confused, and exhilarated by the events that transpire—that is fun for me.

So while any individual has his or her own tastes, attitudes, and predispositions—what confuses me may not confuse you, what excites me may well bore you—but we all define the basic elements of fun in a similar way.

Let's Start with a Simple Element: *Anticipation*.

What would this mean in an e-learning program? It means that your user really wants to see the next screen. He wants to see how it turns out. Now I realize that for some e-learning designers this concept is so foreign it is hard to see what I am saying here. But for a movie maker or a novelist, this is not an odd idea. Consider the phrase "page-turner" in two of its more common uses:

- That novel was a real page-turner.
- The e-learning program was just a page-turner.

So the idea is simple. Build a program where you can't wait to get to the next page to see what will happen there, not one where all you do is turn pages mindlessly.

"And how do I do that?" you ask?

In order for one to anticipate what will happen next, something has to be happening in the first place. Movies have a story line, with characters who have goals and events that thwart those goals. The same would be true in a good e-learning program.

So at the beginning of the design of any good e-learning program, there has to be a character with whom the user can identify and there must be a set of goals that this character is trying to accomplish. Notice that this is exactly what happens in a good video game as well. You either identify with the character who is shooting down incoming aircraft or you don't. If you do, the game is working for you.

> *To build a program where you can't wait to get to the next page to see what will happen there, there has to be a character with whom the user can identify and there must be a set of goals that this character is trying to accomplish.*

Take Another Basic Element of Fun: *Emotional Identification*

Because emotional identification is so important, it is worth spending some time on it here. I cannot tell you how many different e-learning programs I have seen that start with something like: "You have been hired by a large company as its new sales director. You are about to go to an important meeting with your direct reports. The first thing you should say at the meeting is a, b, c, or d.

This is pretty dull stuff, and it is everywhere in e-learning. Why doesn't it work? I have already mentioned why having people choose from a list of things to say is of no value at all, but more than that is problematic here. Who cares about this character? You can tell me that I have been hired by this company and that this is my job, but I haven't and it isn't.

So how do we create emotional identification? Well, how do they do it in the movies? They do not assert that you are a character. In fact, you aren't a character. But if they do their job well, you start to care about the characters and begin to believe that one of them is a lot like some aspect of you. They do this slowly, by having interesting things happen that first cause you to be confused or curious about what is going on. This confusion makes you wonder what will happen next. If it is done well, after a while you are excited and exhilarated by the events that transpire.

This is what e-learning must be like if it is to be fun. Your character, in this case the user, must be placed in a world that is somewhat confusing, where events are taking place and where his or her goals are being thwarted in some way. He or she must be forced to make decisions whose effects make things better or worse for him or her in the scenario. In other words, it has to seem real and the events must relate to concerns that the person actually has in the real world. It can't be about shooting down planes because that is not his or her job. But it can be about people yelling at him or emergencies that need decisions, or people who won't cooperate with her goals, or characters who are working against him or her. This stuff really happens in the workplace and it has to happen in your e-learning program as well. And it needs to happen visually, in such a way that it looks realistic. You can't say, "You are in a room and people are laughing at you," and expect anyone to care. People really need to be laughing at some decision you just made, in order for you to get upset and begin to become engaged in what is going on. That engagement is what e-learning must be about if it is to work at all.

> *For e-learning to be fun, the user must be placed in a world that is somewhat confusing, where events are taking place and where his or her goals are being thwarted in some way.*

Fun and engagement are pretty much the same thing in my view. Engagement just doesn't happen because an e-learning designer wills it to be so, any more than good movies are made just because someone wrote a script.

Why Not Take a Tip from the Movies?

Now I am not suggesting that you need to go into the movie business. But I am suggesting that many people have worked on storytelling before you started on e-learning so there is much to be learned from them.

Here are some (edited) tips for movie makers that I found on a site called funkyfresh.com:

> *"Whether you're creating a two-hour epic or a two-minute news piece, think of your audience as very busy people who want you to get to the point. When it comes to video, if you can make your finished product feel like it's shorter in duration than it actually is, you're a genius (or at least well on your way to being a good filmmaker).*
>
> *"So how do you cheat time? As lounge hip-hop act Mr. Scruff might say, 'You better keep movin.' Everything in your video should have some sort of purpose.*
>
> *"Don't confuse camera movement or montage (a series of related shots) with keeping your story moving. Ask yourself, 'How does this inform and excite the viewer?' Good storytelling with the proper elements usually wins out over bad storytelling with special effects.*
>
> *"One of the most underutilized and often abused elements in home video production is sound, particularly 'natural sound.' Natural sound is the sound of the environment in which you are shooting. It could be anything: a group of people talking, the city streets, or dice rolling on a craps table. For example, if you were shooting a movie about baseball, you'd want to hear the crack of the bat, the pop of the catcher's glove, and maybe some guy yelling 'Peanuts!'*

"Next, think about the pacing of your work. How do you get from your introduction to your closing? Do you spend enough time or too much time explaining things literally? Are there points where an interview seems to go on too long?

"You've probably had to sit through exposition in movies. This is when one character tells another what's going on, and the information's really for the audience, not the character. It's usually the sign of a bad film when the story's so weak the characters have to spell out the plot. This is a technique to avoid.

"Presenting a story in such a way that the viewer can interpret the subtext and draw any number of conclusions can be a lot more interesting than spelling it out. As you lead your viewers on this journey, they'll appreciate your subtlety.

"Tell several stories at once and have them intertwine at the end."

How relevant is this advice to the e-learning designer? Perhaps you think you are not telling a story. Maybe you aren't, but if that is the case no one is going to have fun using your program. Storytelling, as I have said, is at the heart of understanding, which in turn is at the heart of learning.

So if you are telling a story, then pacing, use of visuals and sound, plot lines, and such are all part of it.

Storytelling is at the heart of understanding, which in turn is at the heart of learning. Just make sure the user is really inside the story, determining how events transpire, to create the emotional identification, confusion, determination, and so on that cause people to become engaged in what they're doing.

Of course it would be a mistake to get so into the story-telling that you forgot what the learning was to be about. Unlike movies, the results of an e-learning program should not be predetermined. How it all turns out must be up to the user. Of course many designers ignore this principle. No matter what you do in their programs there is some ending scene that says. "Congratulations you have made a successful sale; now you must decide how to reward the team" or some such nonsense that has nothing whatever to do with the decisions the user actually made in the course of the e-learning program.

Use the storytelling concept, but make sure the user is really inside the story, determining how events transpire. Doing this creates the emotional identification, confusion, determination, and so on that cause a user to get engaged in what he or she is doing.

I realize that this sounds easy and is in fact very hard. Building high-quality e-learning is not easy at all. It requires enough people with enough different specialties that enable the creation of a high-quality production.

But, that having been said . . .

e-Learning Really Doesn't Have to Be Movie-Like at All

When money became less available we could no longer build high-quality movie-like experiences so we settled for high-quality stories that were told in a different medium.

I described the story-centered curriculum at Carnegie Mellon University's West Coast Campus in Chapter 12. Is it fun? Here is an article written on the first graduation of the first totally learning-by-doing class at CMU WCC:

"WEST COAST CAMPUS CELEBRATES FIRST GRADUATING CLASS

"Carnegie Mellon's West Coast Campus in Silicon Valley held its first graduation ceremony on Friday, Aug. 29, on the grounds of Building 17 at the NASA Ames Research Park at Moffett Field, California. Seventeen students received master's degrees in information technology with specializations in software engineering, e-business technology, and the learning sciences.

"Established in September 2001, the West Coast Campus is the university's first branch. Its programs stress the importance of learning by doing and are designed to provide an educational experience that closely simulates the real-world work environment for which students are preparing.

"All of the programs involve extensive, in-depth projects that students complete as teams. This collaborative approach is one of the defining characteristics of Carnegie Mellon's West Coast Campus and has been touted by students as one of the program's most beneficial aspects.

"'What I enjoyed most about my experience at the West Coast Campus were the opportunities to learn with and from my fellow students,' said software engineering student Townsend Duong. 'I found that being part of a close-working team of intelligent individuals who can take the initiative on accomplishing objectives and work out sound solutions is far more valuable than having industry experience or certification of any kind.'

"During this past semester, students completed real-world projects in several areas.

"One group of software engineering students worked with the SAP Corporate Research Center in Palo Alto to complete two projects—one involving two students who

worked collaboratively on a project using animated inter-face agents for e-commerce applications, the second involving three students who worked as a team to build a next-generation multimodal future store framework and integrated it with SAP's Retail Store backend systems.

"'Our project with SAP has been one of the most positive aspects of the program in that it's provided exposure and given us the opportunity to apply what we learned at an established company,' said software engineering student Ju-kay Kwek. 'It's an example of Carnegie Mellon making the most of its name and industry contacts to provide access and value to its students.'

"Other software engineering students worked on Carnegie Mellon's NASA-sponsored High-Dependability Computing Project, a $23.3-million program created to address the agency's ability to design and build highly dependable mission-critical computing systems. Here, students focused on testbeds, or collaborative environments that bring researchers together to conduct experiments related to dependability. They worked to develop a technology that will facilitate construction, deployment, and use of further testbeds.

"In a project with Patroline Air Service, e-business technology students built a prototype of an automated incident reporting system. Consisting of an in-cockpit tablet PC, the system uses digital imaging, real-time GPS/GIS mapping, and workflow automation technologies to improve the effectiveness with which pilots report any observed adverse pipeline conditions to Patroline's customers. Students pilot-tested the prototype and presented an implementation plan to Patroline's management.

"'The projects I completed in Carnegie Mellon's e-business program have had a direct effect on what I've been doing for Patroline,' said e-business technology student

Erick Tai. 'This is what's so different about Carnegie Mellon's West Coast Campus, and this is what makes this project-based learning so much more fulfilling than the traditional classes that we are used to.'

"A learning sciences student working with RoboCamp-West, a college-credit course aimed at high school juniors and seniors, observed the activities of the seven-week program and used what she observed to make recommendations on how to translate the curriculum into an online format. A second learning sciences student developed online performance support materials and course content to help master's level students working at a distance.

"After graduation from the West Coast Campus program, some students will continue their education in doctoral programs, while others plan on entering the workforce.

"'I have high hopes for the future, and I think that this program has offered so many options to me,' said Tai. 'Whereas previously I was just an electrical/computer engineer, I now feel like I can handle just about anything. Carnegie Mellon's West Coast Campus has been quite amazing for me. It's been a great program, and I don't think I'd trade it for any other.'"

Did our students have fun? I think they did. They worked very hard but they were engaged. At times they were confused, but they were determined and exhilarated and excited and fascinated as well. There were no movies and there were no fancy e-learning videos. But what they were doing was all on the web and all mentored online.

Can e-learning be fun? It better be or it won't be around long.

◊   ◊   ◊

Jump Start Your Training

Some Ways to Make e-Learning . . .

Boring

Make people read lots of text onscreen.

Insert long speeches by officials of the company.

Introduce activities with cutesy animation.

Ask questions that have multiple-choice answers.

Tell people that they got the answer wrong.

Ask people to play a game.

Tell them their score in the game.

Set up situations that are unrealistic.

Set up situations that bear no relation to the life of the trainee.

Make sure there is no emotion in any scenario.

Fail to allow employee to practice a skill.

Don't let the employee actually get better at anything.

Fun

Use visually based situations, not text.

Use just-in-time stories from experts when an employee makes a mistake.

Animation must be part of the story the employee is involved in.

Give people a choice of actions.

Bad choices must result in bad consequences that are obvious to the trainee.

Have employees practice things they will actually do on the job.

Define success in training the same way it would happen on the job.

Only use realistic job-like scenarios that an employee would recognize as something that would or could happen to him or her.

The scenarios must be believable and it should feel bad to do badly.

Employees must be able to see their own improvement on the job because of the training.

14

I Disagree
with the Question

The importance of getting questions right—
so the rest of your job is easy

As I mentioned in Chapter 13, I originally worked in the field of Artificial Intelligence (AI). I was a member of the Stanford AI lab at the very beginnings of the field and then set up and ran my own laboratory at Yale for many years.

I worked on getting computers to understand typewritten English. Although today we have the illusion that computers must understand some English—there is Google after all, and it seems to understand something—this can make us wonder about what it means to understand. I (or more accurately the students in my lab) wrote programs that read newspaper articles and paraphrased them, translated them into other languages, and answered questions about them. So the computer seemed to understand something.

Philosophers quibbled about what it meant to understand and asked whether my programs would understand a man asking a woman to dinner as a desperate longing for love. My view was that I was just trying to get computers to be easier to deal with. I thought English was better than FORTRAN or C+ as a means of communication with computers, at least for the average guy. And there was so much text to read. It would have been of great use if computers could get the gist of what they read. But when you use the word "understand" you are subject to attack within the academic world, as I soon found out. I was no philosopher. I was simply trying to solve a hard problem.

I became curious about how the mind worked. There were working minds after all (human ones), and they understood English, so maybe computers could copy what they did, if only we could figure out what that was. So I looked carefully at what people seemed to be doing when they understood or produced a sentence in English.

What I found was that when I asked hard questions about how people did seemingly simple things, like saying what was on their minds, that the processes that seemed to be in operation were very different from those that the well-known philosophers, psychologists, and linguists of the time had figured was the case. In other words, with the exception of some folks in AI who were asking similar questions and some psychologists who ran experiments on people to see whether what I was saying about how people worked was right (it seemed to be!), the linguistics folks found me most annoying. They were writing grammars and I was writing computer programs, which, curiously, didn't need their grammars. They didn't like this state of affairs at all.

When I asked hard questions about how people did seemingly simple things like saying what was on their minds, the processes that seemed to be in operation were very different from those that the well-known philosophers, psychologists, and linguists of the time had figured were the case.

One philosopher who was wondering about whether these AI people had anything to say about the mind wound up moderating a debate (in 1978) between the major antagonists. Here is some of what he had to say about that debate (years later):

WHEN PHILOSOPHERS ENCOUNTER AI*

Daniel C. Dennett

"Philosophers have been dreaming about AI for centuries. . . . When philosophers set out to scout large conceptual domains, they are as inhibited in the paths they take by their sense of silliness as by their insights into logical necessity. And there is something about AI that many philosophers find off-putting—if not repugnant to reason, then repugnant to their aesthetic sense.

"This clash of vision was memorably displayed in a historic debate at Tufts University in March of 1978, staged, appropriately, by the Society for Philosophy and Psychology. Nominally a panel discussion on the foundations and prospects of Artificial Intelligence, it turned into a tag-team rhetorical wrestling match between four heavyweight ideologues: Noam Chomsky and Jerry Fodor attacking AI, and Roger Schank and Terry Winograd defending. Schank

Daedalus, *Proceedings of the American Academy of Arts and Sciences*, 117, 283–295, Winter 1988. Reprinted in S. Graubard (Ed.), *The Artificial Intelligence Debate: False Starts, Real Foundations.* Cambridge, MA: MIT Press, 1988.

was working at the time on programs for natural language comprehension, and the critics focused on his scheme for representing (in a computer) the higgledy-piggledy collection of trivia we all know and somehow rely on when deciphering ordinary speech acts, allusive and truncated as they are. Chomsky and Fodor heaped scorn on this enterprise, but the grounds of their attack gradually shifted in the course of the match. It began as a straightforward, 'first principles' condemnation of conceptual error—Schank was on one fool's errand or another—but it ended with a striking concession from Chomsky: it just might turn out, as Schank thought, that the human capacity to comprehend conversation (and more generally, to think) was to be explained in terms of the interaction of hundreds or thousands of jerry-built gizmos—pseudo-representations, one might call them—but that would be a shame, for then psychology would prove in the end not to be 'interesting.' There were only two interesting possibilities, in Chomsky's mind: psychology could turn out to be 'like physics'—its regularities explainable as the consequences of a few deep, elegant, inexorable laws—or psychology could turn out to be utterly lacking in laws, in which case the only way to study or expound psychology would be the novelist's way (and he much preferred Jane Austen to Roger Schank, if that were the enterprise).

"A vigorous debate ensued among the panelists and audience, capped by an observation from Chomsky's MIT colleague, Marvin Minsky, one of the founding fathers of AI, and founder of MIT's AI Lab: 'I think only a humanities professor at MIT could be so oblivious to the third interesting possibility: psychology could turn out to be like engineering.'

"Minsky had put his finger on it. There is something about the prospect of an engineering approach to the mind that is deeply repugnant to a certain sort of humanist, and it has little or nothing to do with a distaste for materialism or science."

I found out in that debate that I was an engineer, not a scientist. I was interested in the details of how it all worked, not in the fundamental scientific principles that would tie it all together in a neat academic paper. Calling someone an engineer seems to be a bad thing to say about someone in the academic world. So, sad to say, apparently I am a bad guy because I like to hope my work will have some use. I was just trying to figure out some things about the mind that would help me build some useful stuff.

But I had stepped on a few toes. The questions I was asking were certainly about practical things such as how to get computers to be easier to deal with, which offended no one, but they were also about the very nature of what it means to understand, which is, after all, the turf of many serious players in the academic world.

As I see it with the hindsight of many years . . .

The Problem Is with the Questions Rather Than with the Answers

In that debate years ago, we weren't so much talking past each other as much as we were simply asking different questions. I asked: *How does the mind process language?* because I wanted to copy what it did. Chomsky was asking different questions about scientific principles that left me, and still leave me, cold.

I mention all this because defining the right question is a whole lot more important than figuring out the answers. These days there are many people talking about education and talking about training. The real issue is what questions they are asking.

Questions change over time. This is the important point. Because a question was pertinent at one time it does not necessarily follow that we must keep asking it. Times change. The question I was asking, in the late Sixties and Seventies, about how computers could process English, seemed like a good question at the time. It was so hard to use computers in those days. If you could just talk to them! And computers didn't know much in those days. If we could just figure out how computers could know enough, they might be able to answer questions that we wanted to ask. I found those kinds of research questions to be thrilling.

> *Defining the right question is a whole lot more important than figuring out the answers.*

But today these questions hardly make sense. The article that I cited above I found on Google in a minute or two by typing in the right key words. Had I asked the question in English, it really wouldn't have made my life (or the computer's life) all that much easier. Those research questions were great then, but they aren't now. Computers still don't understand, nor do they process English very well. But they really don't have to. The world has changed, and with it the relevant research questions. Good research questions reflect the times in which those questions are asked. Mistakes occur when we still use answers that were composed to questions that no longer make sense.

This is, of course, the problem that we face in education. We are asking the wrong questions and have been asking wrong questions for quite some time. Today's questions are about test scores and learning management systems and what today's students don't know and student-teacher ratios. They are simply out-of-date.

> *Good research questions reflect the times in which those*
> *questions are asked. Mistakes occur when we still use*
> *answers that were composed to questions that no longer*
> *make sense.*

There is a wonderful movie called *Ferris Bueller's Day Off* that reveals a great deal about education. I often use a clip from that movie when I give speeches on education or training wherein the teacher drones on about the Smoot Hawley tariff and George H.W. Bush's view of Reagan's *Voo Doo Economics* while the students doze off. At a different point in the same movie, the lead character blows off a European History test saying:

> *"It's on European socialism. I mean, really! What's the*
> *point? I'm not European . . . I don't plan on being Euro-*
> *pean. So who gives a crap if they're socialists? They could be*
> *fascist anarchists . . . It still wouldn't change the fact that I*
> *don't own a car!"*

What questions were the designers of this test on history or the economics lecture asking? And what questions is Ferris Bueller (or any modern high school student) asking?

Here are two questions we might ask about education:

How Do People Learn?
What Do People Need to Learn?

While these questions seem reasonable enough, they really aren't asked all that often.

Let's imagine Ferris in his European History class. What questions did the designers of that class ask themselves that led them to create the European Socialism test?

If they asked how people learn, then their answer must have been—*by reading and cramming and by listening when the teacher speaks.* If they asked what high school students need to learn, then their answer must have been—*European History.*

Unfortunately, research into human learning makes it clear that neither of these two answers is particularly clever. People learn best when they are pursuing goals that they really care about (which is why Ferris mentions getting a car) and when what they learn directly helps them attain their goals. The best means of learning has always been experience. Philosophers for centuries have commented on this and supported the idea that learning by doing is the most effective means of making something your own. If you wanted to learn about European History the best means would not be listening and reading but doing (the designer needs to figure out what that might mean). If you wanted to achieve some goal that knowing European History would help you achieve, then you might be motivated to know about it.

> *People learn best when they are pursuing goals that they really care about and when what they learn directly helps them attain their goals. The best means of learning has always been experience.*

It is not my goal here to explain how best to teach history. I simply want to point out that the designers of the European History curriculum simply could not have asked themselves these questions. They didn't ask how students learn nor did they ask what their students wanted to learn. Instead they asked different questions. These were

- Given that we have been told to teach European History, how might we do that?
- Given that we have hired a teacher to stand up in front of a class, what might he or she actually say?

Now those aren't very interesting questions. They are simply implementation questions. They presume the answers to an entirely different set of questions that were asked a long time ago. It was decided that European History should be taught to students in American high schools by a committee chaired by Charles Eliot, the president of Harvard, in 1892. Here are the questions that President Eliot asked about how to teach each subject that he had determined should be taught:

1. *"In the school course of study extending approximately from the age of six years to eighteen years—a course including the periods of both elementary and secondary instruction—at what age should the study which is the subject of the Conference be first introduced?*

2. *"After it is introduced, how many hours a week for how many years should be devoted to it?*

3. *"How many hours a week for how many years should be devoted to it during the last four years of the complete course; that is, during the ordinary high school period?*

4. *"What topics, or parts, of the subject may reasonably be covered during the whole course?*

5. *"What topics, or parts, of the subject may best be reserved for the last four years?*

6. *"In what form and to what extent should the subject enter into college requirements for admission? Such questions as the sufficiency of translation at sight as a test of knowledge of a language, or the superiority of a laboratory examina-*

tion in a scientific subject to a written examination on a text-book, are intended to be suggested under this head by the phrase 'in what form.'

7. *"Should the subject be treated differently for pupils who are going to college, for those who are going to a scientific school, and for those who, presumably, are going to neither?*

8. *"At what stage should this differentiation begin, if any be recommended?*

9. *"Can any description be given of the best method of teaching this subject throughout the school course?*

10. *"Can any description be given of the best mode of testing attainments in this subject at college admission examinations?"*

What is most striking about these questions are the presuppositions contained within them about what school was to be about. School was about a course of study of some academic discipline. This went without saying. So no matter what the subject to be studied, Ferris Bueller was going to find himself preparing to be a scholar of some sort, despite the fact that he had no interest whatsoever in becoming a scholar. He and other high school students would have no say in the matter. Their interests were not considered. Their goals did not matter. Charles Eliot knew what their goals should be. He knew what was best for them. And more than 100 years later, no one has bothered to ask if President Eliot had a clue. We simply assume he was right and worry ourselves to death that Ferris has failed his European History exam.

What questions might the committee have asked. Here is one that was definitely not asked: *What subjects should be studied?* The reason that this question was not asked is that the president of Harvard already knew the answer. The subjects would be the ones that were taught at Harvard at that time. There were departments of mathematics, history, English, science, and so on at Harvard in 1892, so that's what high school students should study. Never mind that there are hundreds of departments at Harvard today. The high school curriculum is almost completely the same as it was then.

The problem here is engineering versus science again, I am afraid. Charles Eliot was not trying to produce productive citizens. He was not asking the engineering question. The engineering question (for school) is:

How Do We Create Individuals Who Can Perform Well in Life and in Our Society?

If he had been an engineer or had taken an engineering approach to education, he would have taught students practical skills and general thinking skills. But he was more concerned with trying to get students ready for Harvard or, failing that, to at least know something of what Harvard students would know. Now why he was doing this we can only guess, but it sure wasn't because he was asking the engineer's questions about outcomes.

Here is an engineer's question about education (in an English course):

How do I get students to be able to produce good sentences (when they write or speak)?

Here is a scientist's question about education (in an English course):

How do I get students to learn how to parse a sentence?

Here is another engineer's question, this time in a science course:

> *How do I get students to understand how to*
> *drive their cars under icy conditions?*

Here is a scientist's question (in a science course):

> *How do I get students to learn to balance*
> *a chemical equation?*

Here is an engineer's question in a math course:

> *How do I get students to learn to handle*
> *their financial lives?*

Here is the scientist's question:

> *How do I get students to calculate logarithms?*

The second of each set were the questions that drove your educational experience in school. The first of each set may or may not have come up. It depends on what kind of school you attended. The issue here is what people need to learn in order to live productive and well-reasoned lives. At least that is my issue. That is my education question. Those who design today's curricula are asking the question (without necessarily realizing it): *How do I get students to be scholars?*

Of course they are not actually asking anything of the sort. They are simply asking implementation questions about a curriculum that was decided on in 1892. My questions are for today's world. The 1892 questions were, at the very least, for the world of 1892. However, unless that was a world in which scholarship was critical for living a meaningful and successful life, I suspect that those questions are more than simply outdated, they are very much the wrong questions to have been asking even then.

So What About Disagreeing with the Question?

The thrust of this book has not been about either AI or education, so it may seem that this is an odd chapter. This book has been, on the surface, about training. But it also has been about knowing how to ask and answer the questions that arise in building good training. To know that one needs to know how to disagree with the question because there are a lot of really bad questions already out there.

> *To build good training you need to know how to disagree with the question because there are a lot of really bad questions already out there.*

The question that seems to underlie most training discussions is: How do we get information to a trainee in the most efficient manner?

But I disagree with this question. And so should you.

Believing that training is essentially the transmission of information would of course allow you, or even encourage you, to ask such a question. It is a real issue to worry about what Ferris knows about Europe only if you assume that it is your job to make Ferris capable of reciting facts about Europe when asked.

But how important is the recitation of facts? Suppose an employee simply did his job well all the time but he could not tell you how he did what he did or why he did what he did? You might think he was not very articulate or reflective, but neither would you want to lose him as an employee.

The school model forces us to ask school-like questions. As long as we see training as some form of schooling, we will inevitably ask those questions. We will ask about what an employee knows and how we can get her to know more. We will write training manuals, or build websites, or send memos, or acquire courses, all of which are intended to tell her more stuff so that she can be even better informed.

But if we fail to use the extant school model, if we ask the engineer's questions and not the scientist's questions, then we can begin to attempt to engineer outcomes.

We can ask what kind of employee we want to create and ask what such an employee would be able to do. We can measure output not input. We would not care about whether an employee could tell us what we told him about his job but simply whether he can execute what we ask of him on the job. We would ask what it is we expect him to be able to do, and we would ask ourselves how we can help him do his job better.

> *As long as we see training as some form of schooling, we will inevitably ask school-like questions. We will ask about what an employee knows and how we can get her to know more, instead of asking what kind of employee we want to create and what such an employee would be able to do.*

In this kind of model, measurement means knowing how to determine whether a job was done right and training means allowing trainees to practice until they get it right. Building practice environments thus becomes the object of training.

This is, of course, quite unlike schooling as it exists today. Very little practice takes place in school. But in any real world where execution matters—sports, child raising, cooking, communication skills, construction—practice is all that matters. One gets better at something by doing it and by reflecting on how to do it better next time.

> *When we stop asking school-like questions, we see that training means allowing trainees to practice until they get it right. Building practice environments thus becomes the object of training.*

So this book is really about how to ask the right questions in training. It is also, of course, about the answers. But the answers are much less important than the questions. When you get the questions right, the rest is easy.

◊　◊　◊

Jump Start Your Training

Bad Questions
- What should we teach new employees?
- What would make employees work harder?
- How can we reduce training costs?
- How can we make use of the classrooms we already have so much invested in?
- How can we avoid hiring full-time instructors?
- Who can we hire to be our full-time instructors?
- How can we assess the intelligence of potential new hires?

- How can we increase throughput in training?
- How can we teach employees faster?
- What piece of technology can we buy that will help us do training better?

GOOD QUESTIONS

- What obstacles exist that cause employees to fail to do their jobs properly?
- How can new hires learn from the mistakes of those who have come before them?
- How can we make training part of the job?
- How can we reconceptualize training so that it isn't something you take time off from work to do?
- How can we hire new employees who hardly need training?
- How can we make tools available to employees that answer their questions as soon as they have them?
- How can we introduce the idea of just-in-time mentoring instead of instruction?
- How do we better understand the goals of employees?
- How do we make use of problems on the job to help us design help?
- How do we get the experts of the company (or the world) online?

15

Corporate Dragons

WHY MOST E-LEARNING YOU ARE LIKELY TO ENCOUNTER
ISN'T VERY GOOD—AND HOW TO RECOGNIZE IT

The president of my company (who also is our chief sales guy—it is a small company) was trying to land a major client. He told him about the SCC, and the client asked for something to read. So he sent him the dragon story (Chapter 11). Here is what the potential client replied:

> "Mike—enjoyed meeting you and talking about Socratic Arts. Can you send me something to share with my team that is a little more practical and speaks to your work with corporate customers. The Dragon story is not relevant to our context."

Oh brother. The Dragon story isn't relevant to the corporate context? Okay. Here is a corporate dragon story (without obvious dragons):

Once upon a time there was a major corporation that was overrun with employees who were unprepared to deal with new technologies and a variety of social issues in the workplace. They didn't understand the new products they were selling and they had no idea how to get along with their fellow employees or how to manage their direct reports. An executive committee decided that human resources should offer a variety of courses to employees to teach them how to deal with these issues. Unfortunately times were bad, so no new money was given to the training department to do this. Instead, human resources was instructed to "put everything on the web" and thereby save enough money to introduce many new courses.

The training department was happy that someone was paying attention to them again, but was mystified about how they were to offer new courses without investing new money. Fortunately for them, every other company in the country seemed to have the same problem. This meant that many entrepreneurial new ventures were spawned overnight, all offering courses for these corporations to use. Without very much money being spent, the corporation could now offer a whole catalogue of courses.

Here is the catalog they decided to offer:

From the XYZ catalog they chose all the courses available in conflict management and customer service:

UNDERSTANDING CONFLICT IN THE WORKPLACE
This course shows why and how conflict arises and illustrates general approaches . . .

MANAGING CONFLICT IN YOUR ORGANIZATION
This course teaches ways to identify and manage conflict while . . .

HANDLING VIOLENCE IN THE WORKPLACE
This course helps learners to spot potential violence and prevent . . .

HANDLING WORKPLACE CONFLICT—FOR EMPLOYEES
Ways to deal effectively with conflict between co-workers and team members . . .

HANDLING WORKPLACE CONFLICT FOR MANAGERS
Ways for managers to deal effectively with conflict in the workplace while avoiding . . .

UNDERSTANDING CUSTOMER LOYALTY
What drives customer loyalty and how to develop a culture that keeps customers . . .

DILEMMAS OF INTERNAL CUSTOMER SERVICE
How to deliver consistent and reliable service to internal customers and link performance . . .

CUSTOMER SERVICE TEAMWORK
Skills and processes for service teams to resolve customer dissatisfaction and recover . . .

LEADING CUSTOMER SERVICE TEAMS
Team leadership concepts and skills for improving customer service include . . .

KEEPING CUSTOMER SERVICE SKILLS STRONG
How to sustain and coach employees' customer service skills, uncover and eliminate barriers . . .

From the QED catalog they chose all the live e-learning courses:

Team Effectiveness/$800.00

Conflict Resolution/$800.00

Critical Chain Project Management/$800.00

Managing Multiple Priorities/$800.00

Project Management: Introduction/$800.00

Project Management: Intermediate/$800.00

Microsoft® Project 2002 Certification: Managing
Multiple Projects/$800.00

Microsoft® Project 2002: Managing a Single
Project/$800.00

Process Improvement and Innovation/$800.00

Project Estimating and Scheduling/$800.00

Project Management for IT Professionals/$1,000.00

Project Management Fundamentals/$800.00

Project Cost Controls/$800.00

Project Quality Management/$800.00

Project Risk Management/$750.00

Project Team Development/$800.00

Strategic Planning for Project Management/$200.00

Project Management Certification /$2,500.00

From the ABC catalogue they chose all ninety-odd
courses from fifteen program areas, ranging from Computer
Basics and Desktop Applications to e-Commerce, Technology Architect, and Soft Skills like Conflict Management,
Negotiation skills, Coaching skills, and Dealer Motivation.

From thenewcorp.com catalogue they chose more than
eight hundred courses:

End User Courses

Basic Desktop Computing/185 Courses

Home and Small Business Applications/65 Courses

Business Skills Development/55 Courses

Technical Courses

Technical Basics/195 Courses

Web Development/75 Courses

Database Administration/35

Systems Administration/20

General Skills/200 Courses

The Executive Committee was very excited. Suddenly there was a catalogue of courses available to all employees that covered every imaginable training need. And what was better, no actual money had been spent on development. Employees could take the courses and only then would anyone have to pay any money. Everyone was delighted at this wonderful turn of events.

Now as it happened, there was a training manager named Harry in this company who was from the old school. He had learned his job by doing it for thirty years. He had moved to the training department to help out because he knew how to do so many different jobs in the company, but he was not an education specialist. He held no degree in e-learning or instructional design. He simply knew how to do stuff. And what he knew he had learned on the job.

Harry wasn't so sure about this enormous new catalogue, so he decided to take some of the courses himself to see what they were like. He wondered what people actually learned in these courses. He first looked at one of the courses from the XYZ Company.

This is what he found describing the course:

MANAGING CONFLICT IN YOUR ORGANIZATION

Course Learning Objects

1. Handling hostility

2. Handling challenges to authority

3. Handling verbal aggression

4. Handling overly assertive behavior

5. Handling complaints and negativity

6. Handling passive-aggressive behavior

7. Handling physical threats and violence

8. Assessing your contribution to the situation

Course Length: 1 hour, 25 minutes

After taking this course, you will be able to

- Use different methods of managing and working with difficult people

- Identify and work with people who demonstrate negativity or hostility in the workplace

- Identify and work with people who exhibit aggressive or contentious behavior in the workplace

- Identify and work with people who are overly assertive or domineering

- Identify and work with people who are chronic complainers

- Identify and work with people who are passive-aggressive and avoid conflict

- Identify and work with people who threaten or engage in physical violence

- Assess your own behavior to understand how it may contribute to conflict in the workplace

Harry wondered what a learning object was. He guessed that this was a fancy name for "module," which was after all another fancy name for "part 1" or "part 2." He noticed that the course lasted 85 minutes and that there were eight learning objects, so he figured that each of them lasted about ten and a half minutes. He wondered what anyone could learn about anything in ten and a half minutes. He noted that there were eight outcomes promised, so he realized that in ten and a half minutes he would be able, at the end of one of the modules, to recognize and deal with employees who are aggressive and contentious in the workplace. Harry figured that would be five and a quarter minutes for recognizing and five and a quarter minutes for dealing with such employees.

Harry had been working in the company for over thirty years, and he had learned that it wasn't always easy to tell who was out to get you or who intended to undermine your work. He had learned a few things in thirty years, but the problem still bothered him. He was very impressed that he could learn how to identify these behaviors in five and a quarter minutes online. He was even more impressed that he would now know how to deal with them after only five and a quarter more minutes. He wondered how XYZ did it. They sure must be smart folks.

Harry thought maybe XYZ was just one of those companies that promised too much. He thought he would look at another set of online offerings, so he chose to view one of the team development courses offered by the QED Company. Harry noted that this was a live e-learning course. He didn't know what that meant exactly, but then he saw that there were four three-hour sessions on particular dates. Harry, being a smart guy, realized that this was really a live class that could be taken at the office on your computer. He was ready to find out more. He looked at the description:

THE HIGH PERFORMANCE TEAM

Tools, Techniques, and Tips for Team Development
In this course, you will learn to select effective team members for critical roles, develop a high-performance team culture, and book performance for quick implementation and superior results . . .

Who Should Attend
Managers, team and project leaders, supervisors, executives, union leaders, program and project managers, anyone aspiring to be a team or project leader

Harry read on. . . . He saw that he would learn all about building effective teams and fostering intra-team participation and support. He would learn recruitment and hiring skills, how to do goal-setting and action planning, how to use different collaboration and consultation methods, and how to sell his ideas to the team and to management. The course blurb also promised that he would develop group facilitation, training, and consensus-building skills, and he would learn how to construction a transition tree.

Harry again was really impressed. This course was twelve hours long and it covered a lot more material than the XYZ course. Harry had been trying to get teams to function for more than the twenty years that he had been a manager in this company. He hadn't found it to be so easy. With the QED course, twelve hours later he would know how to do it. He noted that he would learn how to deliver a training session in those twelve hours and that he would learn to define a milestone and that he would learn how to visualize a goal and that he would find the secrets to selling his ideas.

Harry had never had much trouble defining a milestone or visualizing a goal, but he had been trying to sell his ideas all his life. He was glad that he would now know how to do it. But Harry did wonder who this course was really going to work for. He knew a lot about running teams, so he figured it wasn't really for him. Was it for people who had never run teams? Then how would they understand the issues involved, like trying to motivate a slacker or keeping the loudest guy from dominating everyone or dealing with people who hated each other? He barely knew what to do in these situations. What he did know he had learned from hard experience. He still remembered the time he made a dysfunctional team deliver a proposal at the last minute by making them all to work in separate rooms with him as a go-between. Now he would learn how to do this by constructing a transition tree, whatever that was. Would wonders never cease?

Harry was getting frustrated. He knew the executive committee was happy to have this great catalogue of e-learning courses, but what would anybody actually be learning?

Harry had learned how to deal with difficult employees and run teams by doing it for thirty years. Did these five-minute-long or hour-long shortcuts really teach anybody anything? Don't people need to learn from experience? Maybe the problem wasn't so much with e-learning, Harry thought, as with the whole concept of a course. Why should five and a quarter minutes or even five and a quarter hours teach you anything worth knowing? What Harry had learned in life he had learned from thinking hard about how to deal with problems he was having, by asking the advice of others, by trying new plans of attack, by seeing what worked and what didn't, and then trying again. Could courses really replace this kind of experience?

> *Why should five and a quarter minutes or even five and a quarter hours teach you anything worth knowing?*

Harry decided to look at what the ABC Company offered. There were so many courses there. Maybe they were different. Their courses were very expensive, so he looked to see what they might be like before he ordered any.

He learned that the "courseware" was simply printed books, and the course was built on the principle of "blended learning," which sounded like "self-paced learning" to Harry, combined with a way to resolve questions and concerns through an e-library or online chat support. Each student would receive a login id and password so that he or she could take online assessments for each "chapter." When all chapters are completed, the student takes a final assessment online.

Wow! Harry was amazed. Online learning really meant online assessment. Blended learning, a term he had been wondering about for some time, really meant "read a book, talk about it with your friends, and then we will give you a test online." The training department had used workbooks and CBT for fifteen years before e-learning was even a word. Everyone knew they didn't work. The workbooks were so bad that they were referred to in company parlance by epithets that could be repeated only by using acronyms that replaced the curse words. No one was proud of those workbooks, they just didn't know how to make it better given limited resources. And this was what online learning meant. Back to workbooks! Harry was exasperated. Is this what the Executive Committee really wanted?

Harry took a look at the almost 1,000 courses offered bynewcorp.com. He thought maybe he should consider technical courses instead of the more touchy-feely ones he had been looking at. Here is the first one he found under databases:

ACCESS 2000 MOUS: CREATING DATABASES

Synopsis
Access 2000 MOUS: Creating Databases shows users how to plan and create a database in Access 2000.

Audience
This course is for anyone preparing for the MOUS Access 2000 Core certification exam.

Time
3 hours

An exam preparation course! Well, those have been around for a long time too, Harry thought. Harry knew that no one ever learned to program because he could answer multiple-choice questions about programming. He looked at the other technical courses and saw that they were all exam prep courses. Practice at multiple-choice tests and you will get good at taking them, Harry knew. He also knew that he would never hire anyone whose credentials consisted of tests that he had passed instead of work that he had done.

Harry began to think that maybe he was just seriously out of touch with the modern world. Maybe no one really cared about teaching anyone anything. They just seemed to care about appearing to have taught someone something. He knew this was true of things like "diversity courses," for example. He knew that they were offered so that companies could say they had offered them. Imagine learning tolerance from a course. But no one had ever taken those courses seriously, they were just trying to avoid lawsuits. Everyone knew that, and now that sham model seemed to pervade all training.

> *Maybe the people designing these courses didn't care about teaching anyone anything. Maybe they just cared about appearing to have taught someone something.*

Harry prepared a report for the Executive Committee. He said that the courses he had seen were a travesty and that the company should not be proud of offering them to employees. He noted that sometimes employees enjoyed taking them, but that that didn't mean they had learned much from them. He suggested that training be eliminated as a function of the company. He thought that since no actual training was being provided that amounted to much, there was hardly any point in wasting time and money on offering it.

> *Just because employees enjoyed taking certain courses didn't mean that they had learned much from them.*

He did add one suggestion to an otherwise depressing report. He suggested that the whole concept of a course needed to be rethought. In its place he suggested that if the company really cared about people learning to deal with complex issues, they should spend some serious time having employees deal with those issues, allowing perhaps whole weeks or longer for employees to deal with simulated experiences that would allow them to, at the very least, not be trying something for the first time when they had to deal with it at work.

> *If the company really cared about people learning to deal with complex issues, they should spend some serious time having employees deal with those issues—weeks, even longer.*

The Executive Committee thanked Harry for the report, but they really weren't sure that they cared all that much about training, at least not enough to have employees spend a long time learning what course offerers said they could learn in five and a quarter minutes. But they did give Harry a special budget line to build one example of what he had in mind.

Harry is now looking for an e-learning company to help him build that example. So far, all he has found are companies who know how to build multiple-choice tests interrupted by pointless animation.

No dragons in this story. Well, no fire-breathing ones anyway. The real dragons in the corporate training world are the CEOs who expect to train people in 85 minutes and the course builders who fail to say "You must be kidding!"

> *The real dragons in the corporate training world are the CEOs who expect to train people in 85 minutes and the course builders who fail to say "You must be kidding!"*

Universities and Companies Actually Have the Same Problems When It Comes to Education

Neither wants to spend very much money on making a high-quality educational experience. Each has people with vested interests inside the organization who want things to remain the same so that they can keep on doing what they have always done. No one really cares whether anyone is learning because no one's job depends on it. Professors aren't judged on how much students learn. They are judged on their publications, their ability to get grants, and whether students think they are good teachers. Since students are mostly concerned with graduating and getting a degree, they are inclined to like teachers who don't make that task too difficult. Universities are the last places that one would expect an attempt to fix education because the customers keep coming back. As long as people vie to get into Harvard, Harvard need not ask whether students are really learning. People go to Harvard, for the most part, for their ability to say they went there for the rest of their lives, not for what they learned while they were there.

But why are things the same in companies? None of the university situation would seem to apply. That is why our potential client said that the Dragon story wasn't relevant to his context.

But companies have inadvertently copied the university model. They provide courses. They suggest how many courses should be taken. They do not seriously check to see whether anyone actually learns anything. They employ staffs who battle against change. They trust certificates supplied by outside vendors who may not really care if anyone has learned anything at all.

What Is to Be Done?

Of course, you know that my answer is the Story-Centered Curriculum. We must endeavor to recreate the experiences we think employees will actually have on the job so that they can have them before they screw up with real customers and real people. The simulation of actual experience does not come cheap. Whether it is done on a computer or in a live simulation or anything in between, it must seem real, it must feel real, and people must be able to screw up, feel bad about it, and have to think hard about what they did wrong. Experts, live or on video, must be there to help when employees get things wrong and there must be no bad consequence to getting things wrong. Creating learn-by-doing experiences is complicated, and going through them takes time. When companies want to spend realistic amounts of time on learning, usually because that learning really matters, they quite often figure out how to do it right.

> *Whether a simulation is done on a computer or live or anything in between, it must seem real, it must feel real, and people must be able to screw up, feel bad about it, and have to think hard about what they did wrong.*

And if they can't figure it out for themselves, they can always ask us for help.

◊   ◊   ◊

Jump Start Your Thinking

How can you know if the e-learning you are being offered by an e-learning provider is likely to not be very good?

Some hints . . .

The Course Catalog Is Too Big

Think about it. When an e-learning company has hundreds of courses to offer, how much money could they have invested in building them? When we were building simulation-based courses, it cost us about $100,000 to build each hour of instruction. Now that we are building story-centered mentored courses, it costs about $5,000 per hour of instruction. Imagine if we had a course catalogue of 100 courses. Given that it takes at least ten to twenty hours to learn anything of much use, that would mean that the expensive method would cost between $1 million and $2 million to build and the cheaper method would cost $50,000 to $100,000 to build. If our simulation company offered 100 courses, that means we would have had to have had $100 million to invest in development, at least. For the current cheaper method, we would have needed $5 to $10 million of investment. While there was plenty of money around from venture folks in the old days (for the simulation stuff) and there is less now (for the cheaper stuff), either way the numbers I just cited are way too high for the richer times and way too high for now.

What does this mean? It means that what is being offered by the e-learning companies is text on screen followed by a test. Worthless junk. No simulations. No doing. No mentoring. No figuring things out for yourself. No practice. In short, no learning.

The Courses Are Too Short

You simply can't learn to do anything in an hour. Let's imagine I was trying to teach you to hit a softball. I could pitch to you for an hour and give you some advice as you swung. Maybe you would connect with a few balls during that time. But would you feel that now you could hit? You would know better. Learning to hit a softball happens over a lifetime. You get better with years of practice. Without practice, learning simply doesn't take place. I can tell you some things about hitting in an hour. Putting them into practice is a longer-term affair.

The Word *Blended* Is Being Used

Yes, I know "blended learning" is the phrase these days. But think about why it is being used. When is the learning in classrooms and when is it online? Typically, classrooms are used for interactions with people of some sort, so the e-learning part is for the stuff that doesn't need people. Now this could mean practice, which would be good, but the practice I have in mind requires simulations, and if they had simulations they would have had a lot of the people stuff already built in and they wouldn't need classrooms at all.

So the part that is assigned to e-learning is the rote learning part—the facts followed by the answers. That stuff doesn't stick, and for the most part trainees hate it. Other than that, it's great. When you hear "blended"—run.

The Training Is Generic—One Size Fits All

This is the most common problem and in a way the most important. It is tempting for e-learning companies to offer a large catalogue of courses. That is a good way to make money. But who will take those courses? The courses must be created in such a way as to be as applicable to the employees in the airline industry as they are to employees in the banking industry. And they must work just as well for Wachovia as they do for IBM. Now we all know that neither Wachovia nor IBM would use the other's courses. (Trust me, they were both my clients for many years—their problems are different and they aren't into sharing their expertise with the next guy.)

So while big companies build their own training based on their own experts and the situations peculiar to their business and their company, smaller companies try to use the generic stuff. Now sharing with each other is very nice, but it simply won't work in business. Procedures differ from company to company, so there is no way you could share training for procedural matters. Product training needs to be different, obviously. That is why you see generic one-size-fits-all training for Excel or for handling a difficult employee. Presumably these things are the same across companies and therefore the smaller companies can all use the same stuff. Think again.

Excel is only the same out of context. But in reality, Excel is used in real situations, by real people, for real results. Learning how to prepare a business plan for a new product in a given company would involve the use of Excel, but as part of a process that is likely to be company-specific. The trainee doesn't need to learn every feature of Excel, the likely subject of the generic course. Rather, he or she needs to prepare the business plan using Excel, and this is a process that would dwell much less on obscure Excel features and much more on how things are done at the company. Sending the employee off for a quick Excel course isn't likely to be of much use in the scheme of things.

The issue becomes more complex when you are trying to teach problem diagnosis. It may seem that an airline mechanic is doing a job that is quite similar to an automotive mechanic, but no one would think about sending one to a course about the other in the hopes that that will be good enough. We know that such learning transfer doesn't actually take place.

Procedures have to be learned in detail and in context. "General problem solving" is not usually a useful course. But if we know this, why send someone off to a course in dealing with a difficult employee? Difficult people are the same everywhere, I suppose, but each company has different recourses available and different situations that the work environment is likely to cause. Is an employee in a consulting company who is always late the same as a bank teller who is always late? The reasons are likely to be quite different, as are the consequences of the tardiness to the company. One might be a prima donna with unique skills, while the other might have sick children at home. These similar situations really are unlikely to even be related with respect to the proper way to deal with them.

Every company must learn to design its own training for that training to be effective. Off-the-shelf e-learning is certainly cheap, and therefore attractive, but its usefulness is illusory.

16

---+---

Time for AI

HOW AI MIGHT HELP WHEN YOU HAVE A PROBLEM
THAT YOU NEED A SMART COMPUTER TO DO—
LIKE BUILDING STORY-BASED TRAINING SYSTEMS

When my team moved from the Yale Artificial Intelligence (AI) lab to start the Institute for the Learning Sciences at Northwestern in 1989, it was naturally expected that we would develop training systems that were intelligent. We built some very high quality, very influential training systems at ILS, but we didn't try to make them smart. We built some very high quality simulations designed to allow employees to practice different situations before experiencing them in the real world. These were very well received in the commercial world, dramatically changing the way the training world viewed the power of the computer and its potential to help employees learn better. Still, we were AI researchers, so we were constantly asked: "Where is the AI?" At first I found this a very odd question.

Who cared where the AI was as long as we had built some good stuff?

But expectations are pretty powerful things and we were AI researchers, and ILS was this new AI place, so why hadn't we put AI into our teaching systems? Why indeed? Because I was trying to fix some real problems in education. AI was great fun, but I felt it was time to do something that would immediately effect change in a world of education and training that was in serious need of change. I wrote an answer to the "Where is the AI?" question in an *AI Magazine* article that appeared in 1990. It was directed to AI people, not training people, because the question said something about what people expected AI to be. Typically their expectations involved an "oh wow" when the computer did something very cool that you could never believe a computer could do. We had been very good at building such "oh wow" experiences at Yale, so our new corporate observers at ILS expected more.

What I said in the article was that the basic idea of what belonged in a teaching system—the use of simulation, the value of expectation failure, the role of just-in-time storytelling, and proper use of a knowledge base—were AI ideas and that for now we had simply to get those ideas across to an industry that thought computer-based training meant lots of multiple-choice questions that tested whether you had understood what you had just read or seen on the computer. AI is about modeling what people do on a computer. But when we looked at training we saw that trainers had indeed already done just that. Training was mostly about reading and answering questions about what you had read. Training didn't need to be automated, it needed to be radically reconceptualized.

> *When we looked at training we saw that training didn't need to be automated, it needed to be radically reconceptualized.*

So that's what we set out to do, apply the insights that derived from our work in cognitive science, and the technological know-how that derived from our work in AI, to create new models of training, approaches that used computers to provide learning experiences matched to the way humans learn best, rather than using computers to replicate what human trainers were doing. The most important issue at the time was to get those ideas across to the training industry. The best way to do that, we judged, was to build lots of demonstrations by hand. We wanted to show what needed to be done rather than show how smart and clever the computer was that could do it.

To make high-quality training a reality in companies, one needs to build thousands, and maybe millions, of programs, not the one hundred or so that we actually built at ILS. We would have had to create sophisticated technology to automate the process in order to build multiple training systems. The training world did indeed need AI tools, but these would have to wait until the need for them was well understood by the people who would be using them.

Fifteen years later the world has changed. Many companies have come to understand the value of simulations and just-in-time storytelling. It is easy enough to find stories and simulations in your typical e-learning system. (Unfortunately, it is just as easy to find learning objects that tell you what the six principles for doing a job right are, but I digress.) While I do not believe that the role of expectation failure or the proper use of a knowledge base is all that common in e-learning, sometimes one can find that as well. What is missing then? The AI. e-Learning systems are none too smart. It is time.

> *Many companies have come to understand the value of simulations and just-in-time storytelling. What is missing is the AI. e-Learning systems are none too smart.*

HOW WOULD AI IMPROVE TRAINING SYSTEMS?

Let's start by looking at one particular key element of an effective case-based teaching system, which is the presentation of relevant stories (usually in video form) at just the right time—when triggered, for instance, by a mistake that a learner makes in a simulation.

In 1989, we made a decision. We decided to hard wire the stories into the simulation rather than to develop an AI-based scheme for having the simulation system retrieve relevant stories automatically. This meant that, if you made a certain kind of error, you would hear a particular story, one that the developer of the system had decided should be told at that point. The decision to hand-index stories was made because at the time, the size of story databases was severely limited by various pragmatic issues. For example, the video-delivery technology of the day required a clunky jukebox to store even moderate amounts of video. For another, our clients were still shy about committing any stories about mistakes or failure to video. With small or even moderate-sized databases of stories (the biggest was 1,000 or so; usually there were far fewer), the intelligence required for automated indexing and retrieval was not an absolute essential. While our AI selves urged us to dive into these technologies, our pragmatic selves told us that, at that time, this wasn't the best way to direct our resources.

Now things have improved considerably. The success we have had with hand-built systems has helped people understand the value of letting trainees learn from first-person stories told by their best experts at just the right moment in the learning experience. Experts are more willing to tell about mistakes so as to avoid them in the future, and they want to make much larger databases of the war stories available to their learners. On the technology front, there have been several relevant advances: the development of high-speed networks (including the Internet); dramatic reductions in the cost of digital storage; and the emergence of high-quality video compression and delivery standards. This has made the management and delivery of very large video knowledge bases a practical possibility.

> *Successful hand-built systems have helped people understand the value of letting trainees learn from first-person stories told by their best experts at just the right moment in the learning experience.*

Fifteen years ago the key questions were about things like how to elicit the right stories from experts and how a system should present them to be educationally effective. While proper design remains a key issue, important questions about scale and automation have been added. For example . . .

How Does a Company Design and Deliver a Thousand Training Programs a Year that Are High Quality But Nevertheless Relatively Inexpensive to Build?

While this doesn't necessarily seem to be the same thing as asking the question *"How do we make training systems smarter?"* it is. It is rather difficult to build a high-quality training system when all you have is PowerPoint. That much is obvious to most folks in the training industry. What is less obvious is that the same is true of other technologies used for training (like, for example, learning management systems). Whatever the technology you use to build a training system, that technology imposes a theory on the designer. The theory might be simply that there is no theory, that all there is to training is whatever you write on a slide. But that too is a theory—namely that reading what others say will teach you how to do something. Obviously, we don't agree with that theory (nor do we agree with the theory that good training is about knowing what learning objects a students has covered so far), so what theory should be embodied in technology?

> *Whatever the technology you use to build a training system, that technology imposes a theory on the designer.*

The Theory/Technology Question Is Where the AI Answer Becomes Relevant

The theory of learning we propose is simple enough (and I might point out at least as old as Plato—the man, not the computer system). People learn best when they experience a situation, must decide how to deal with issues that arise in that situation, and are coached through their mistakes by experts. So good training tools would help designers build situations that can cause mistakes and provide experts to help. Not surprisingly, this is quite like an AI problem that has been around as long as there has been AI, the problem of getting a computer to act like an expert. In this case that would mean an expert coach who can talk to you about what you just did that was wrong, but the problem is inherently the same.

> *People learn best when they experience a situation, must decide how to deal with issues that arise in that situation, and are coached through their mistakes by experts. So good training tools would help designers build situations that can cause mistakes and provide experts to help.*

THIS IS A CLASSIC AI PROBLEM: GETTING THE RIGHT KNOWLEDGE TO THE RIGHT USER AT THE RIGHT TIME

In AI, initial attempts at this problem in the late Seventies were called expert systems. I objected to how expert systems were constructed and in the early Eighties wrote a book called *Dynamic Memory*, in which I proposed the building of case-based reasoning systems instead. The idea was simply that expertise cannot be modeled by a system of rules (like expert systems), but must be modeled by a collection of cases linked to situations in which they are most applicable. Cases are best expressed as stories, told just in time to someone who is in need of hearing them to help her make a decision. This is called *case-based teaching*.

> *Expertise cannot be modeled by a system of rules (like expert systems), but must be modeled by a collection of cases linked to situations in which they are most applicable.*

We built a number of prototypes in the early Nineties of AI-based training systems that used case-based reasoning technology. While these systems were never fully built (owing in part to our inability to collect full story databases from clients and in part to the technological difficulties of deploying them at that time), the ideas were well enough understood. But the tools to solve them have never been completely finished. Now is the time. But they have to be finished in a context in which they will be used. We must begin to build a set of AI-based training tools to implement case-based teaching.

The Underlying AI Problem That Is the Core of Case-Based Teaching Is Called the *Indexing Problem*

This problem has three parts.

1. What's the Proper Index?

The first part of the indexing problem is determining, in the situation-assessment phase, what the proper index is, that is, what idea is being talked about and what the problem is. Suppose someone chooses to tell a customer what the official policy of the store is when the customer has a complaint and the customer gets angry. This is a situation that calls for a story. Different companies might have different points of view here and thus might want to tell different stories. One company might suggest that customers hate hearing about policies and might propose an alternative explanation. Another might empower the employee to do whatever he or she can to make sure the customer is happy. A third might suggest ways to calm down the customer while sticking to the policy. But all of these stories would have to be retrieved by the same label.

This label would look something like: *angry customer: customer complaint responded to by policy statement*. The item in Italic is an index.

How Does This Index Get There and How Is It Used? Well it doesn't get there by magic. Nor would it get there by any AI system that will exist anytime soon. Having an AI system index a story is a wonderful idea, of course. It is just very hard to do. It would entail having a computer read a given story (watching the video or listening to the audio being almost too hard to contemplate). At first thought, you might imagine that some key words and other statistical information, like they use in Google for example, might be of use, but the fact of the matter is that this really wouldn't help at all. The problem is to figure out the intention of the storyteller, what situation he is describing, what he thinks you should learn from what he said, and why it matters. This stuff is well beyond anything we can expect from AI just now. Oh, we could build a program that did exactly this for a few stories, but for any story the program might ever read? Not right now.

So we are left with hand coding the stories. This is not as hard as it appears. Someone has to record and edit these stories anyway. All we need to index them for use in a case-based teaching system is an indexing tool that makes it easy to do. This we can build. Of course, it helps to have a theory of indexing first, but we have thought long and hard about this over the last twenty years. So the first part of the problem is building the indexing tool that constructs an index from input given by the encoder of the story, like the index above.

Of course, that is not all there is to this part of the problem.

Situations Have Indices Too   In fact, the situation had better have the same index as the story to be told or it won't be found. To index situations, one has to build the simulation properly in the first place. This is where the design issues come in. If the basic structure of the training program is properly designed, then one of its basic elements would be the situation-response template. A situation is set up, and possible responses on the part of the user are enabled. For each one of these pairs, an index is automatically constructed. This can be done if the basic structure of the program has been compiled by a tool that, in allowing the developer to put in a situation and a set of responses, also calls for descriptors of the intent of each situation and response. These would all be written in the same indexing language, of course. So when inserting the "angry customer" video as a response to an action, that label becomes part of the index to be completed when the user selects an action. If the action she selects is to respond with a policy statement, then assuming that response has been labeled in that way, voila, we have the index.

Now if you have been following this, and I am sorry if it seems a little complicated, then you might have realized that the index I gave above, while adequate as a way of labeling the situation, may not be adequate at all for labeling the story to be told. This leads to part two of the indexing problem.

2. How Best to Retrieve the Story?

Part two involves retrieving the proper story from the story database using the index that has been encoded. This is easy to do when the index that we need: *angry customer: customer complaint responded to by policy statement* happens to be the index of the story that is most appropriate. But, as I will explain, it rarely is that simple.

Let us imagine that we have a story in our database that tells about a customer service person who always quoted company policy and how sales in the store he worked in fell as soon as he arrived and rose as soon as he left. The message in the story is that company policy should never be told to angry customers because it really annoys them. We might very well have labeled that story as *angry customer: customer complaint responded to by policy statement* and everything would be hunky dory.

But suppose we had labeled that story as *employee hurts company with bad attitude* or *customer service is about being of service* or *poor uses of psychology in our store* or *knowing when to override a company policy*. No, you might say, those don't look like indices. (They don't, but they could be written so that they did.) Or you might say, the indexing language would prevent writing indices like that. (It could prevent it, but it shouldn't.)

Why are these fine indices? Because indices really need to be about the point of a story. It is the point of a story that drives us to tell it, after all. But some stories have many possible points. Consider the "Roadrunner" cartoons. There is always the point that a coyote can't outrace a roadrunner, but he can't outwit him either. And sometimes the point is about the proper use of TNT or the mysterious appearance of trains running through imaginary train tunnels. Good stories have lots of points. That is my point, but of course, it is not my only point.

The lesson from this is simple. A story may have been recorded from an expert because you have a particular situation in a training program that requires a story and you asked the questions that would elicit exactly the story you wanted. But over time this makes for an impossible situation. It means that stories cannot be re-used, even though they might be relevant, because the program would never say, "Hey, how about that story we used before? That would be pretty good here too." In fact, with enough stories, no human would ever find them either, because no one person would have heard them all (or remembered them). So the key issue is the creation of a story database, but as the number of stories in this database grows very large, it becomes impossible to find them when you might need them.

> *Indices really need to be about the point of a story. It is the point of a story that drives us to tell it, after all. But some stories have many possible points. We want the computer to know what story to tell in response to the situation. This is a job for AI.*

We want the computer to simply know what story to tell in response to the situation. This is a job for AI. To make this magic happen . . .

Two Things Are Required   First, the encoder of the stories must have an indexing tool that is flexible enough to allow her to index the stories multiple times in multiple ways for creating multiple points. To do this, the tool must embody a theory of points that can be made in any given context. Then with these multiple labeled stories available to a computer that can retrieve based on these labels, situations must be labeled not only with respect to what the situation is about but also with respect to what the company that is building the training program wants to say about the proper behavior in that situation.

In other words, the design tool not only requests a label for the situation but also asks the developer to say what the right thing would be to do in that situation. This is all said in the indexing language, of course. Then, and here is the AI, the AI program would find the proper story for use in that training program.

> *AI, by my definition here, is simply the proper representation of the nonconscious knowledge that people employ when they accomplish various mental feats. Finding the right story at the right time to tell is, of course, one of those amazing mental feats. People do not know how they do it, they simply do it. In AI, our job is to figure out what they are doing and represent it in such a way that the computer can do the same kinds of things.*

The computer finds and tells stories that correspond best to the situation at hand and to the teaching intentions of the developers of the software. So that there would be no surprises, the developer might look to see what stories are being told. Of course, the developer might never see what actually happens after she has come to trust what the computer says, because, as the story database is added to over time, the responses would in fact not be surprising after a while.

Of course, none of this makes sense to do if there is no story database that is constantly expanding over time. We do not really have expanding story databases now, but we will soon have to have them. One of the reasons we don't have them now is that no one has understood why they were needed and if anyone has understood, he hasn't known how to build them in such a way as to keep them manageable. But if a large company wants to really deal with managing its corporate knowledge and delivering that knowledge just in time, such expanding, manageable story databases are quite important. As long as each individual training program can be handcrafted, we do not need this AI approach to training. But when the need for course assembly lines is recognized, and this will more and more be the case as companies begin to take training seriously, these AI issues will not be far behind.

3. How to Redirect the Conversation

The third part of the AI problem is determining how to redirect the conversation, or simulation, depending on the story that has been retrieved. It is all well and good to tell a good story. A trainee will be happy to hear about something that is germane to a problem she is having in a simulation for example, or perhaps to one that she is having on the job. Good stories are entertaining and enlightening when they are told to an audience that is especially ready for them. A good AI-based training program should be able to do exactly that. But then what?

Stories don't exist out of context. If you take them from another context, and indeed I am suggesting that that is exactly what will happen, they are still heard as if they were in context. A story not only makes a point, therefore, it also suggests a course of action to someone who is in a decision-making situation. When the trainee chooses a course of action and is interrupted by a story, some things will have already happened in the software. The program will have decided that the action taken was wrong in some way and will have decided that there is a good point to be made about the action that was taken. It will also have decided that some new strategy should be considered inside the training program. If the trainee pilot crashed the plane, for example, after telling a good story about the mistake that was made, the program would want to set up the same situation again. If the trainee angered a customer, the course of action might be to now attempt to calm the customer down. Or it might be to set up the situation again, as with the pilot. There are many other courses of action that a program can initiate besides "do it again" and "deal with the mess you made," but those are two common ones. Others are "let's discuss why you did that," "what other choices might you have made?" "let's try something simpler," and so on. I assume you get the idea.

THE ISSUE HERE IS GOOD TEACHING STRATEGY, AND THIS TOO IS AN AI PROBLEM

How one chooses from various courses of action in a training program depends on many factors, not the least of which is how many alternatives have been built into the program in the first place. The good news is that, done right, these things need not be handcrafted for each training situation. Discussing how you made a decision or how to deal with faulty actions can be modules that exist independently of the particular training program that is being used. Dealing with angry people is a module that can exist outside of any one program, for example. A user could be thrown into that module by a wise teaching program that told a good story that changed the focus of the program from what was being taught to what now has to be taught given the trainee's actions. A good teacher teaches what the student needs to know, regardless of whether that was in fact the original intention of the training. Of course, you would want the module to know what had happened prior to entry in that module, and this is again an issue of knowledge representation and effective use of the available knowledge about the domain, teaching, the point of the story, and so on.

> *A good teacher teaches what the student needs to know regardless of whether that was in fact the original intention of the training. A wise teaching program would tell a good story that changed the focus of the program from what was being taught to what now has to be taught given the trainee's actions.*

CAN WE REALLY DO ALL THIS?

I think so. Many of these problems were understood well enough ten years ago, but the technology was not ready. Also those who were in need of high-quality dynamic training systems had not yet understood this need.

Now we are ready. We can store thousands of stories. We can retrieve them as needed. And those who need training systems are better informed about the need for nontrivial systems that contain a wealth of knowledge and deliver different information to different users depending on their needs. The time for building two-hour training systems that say the same thing to every user has passed. Now it is time to build dynamic story-based systems that converse with users about real problems they are having in real life (at home or at work) or in a simulation and that provide up-to-date and changing answers depending on the complexity and dynamic nature of the story database that comprise the knowledge that a company (or a society) collectively owns.

There Are Many Possible Uses for This Kind of AI Technology in Training

One application that is easy to describe is an enormous database that users can simply ask questions or describe a problem they are having and engage that system in a dialogue that is pertinent to solving their problem. This requires an AI story base that can interact with users by understanding their needs and getting the expertise (in the form of video stories) to them. But there are other uses as well.

When an employee is about to go out into the real world, for example on a sales call, it is a good idea for him or her to be very familiar with the situation about to be encountered. Training that takes place weeks or months before the actual event will be forgotten. This means, in effect, practicing that situation just prior to the sales call with the help of experts. So if a salesperson is about to call on a small business that is owned and operated by a family, it is important for him or her to hear from experts on that situation and then practice a sales call in a simulation of a situation as close as possible to the one about to be encountered. This is not an issue of learning general principles. It is simply one of practicing in as similar an environment as can be constructed with experts who know about that environment, as specifically as possible, who can help the salesperson through the simulated call.

But how would this simulation come to exist? There are enough situations in a large company that it is unreasonable to expect that a simulation would have been built for each possible need of every employee. This would be way too expensive, too time-consuming for the training department to build, and simply unlikely to happen.

The solution to this problem is to build a generic sales call simulator tool that will allow the learning specialists at a company to add the specifics of a given environment as needed. Thus, the simulator tool would allow for the construction of specific simulations by treating the data about the particular sales call as variables that can be added by learning specialists as needed.

Expertise Could Be Added in Three Ways

One would be the data about a given type of company and sales call that a company would add each time it constructed the particular situation. This data would, in effect, create many different simulations, each for different data.

The second kind of data would be the company expertise about products and situations like the one being addressed, in video form that would be put in a case base and indexed automatically to key points where mistakes might be made in the simulation.

The last type would be very practical data about the target company that a company would have in its records that would be added as textual material to familiarize the employee with the real in-depth particulars. This data would come from an archive of previous calls created for this purpose. All this works together to produce particular sales call practice situations for new products or for established customers, without having to specially construct it each time.

Another Use of the Dynamic AI Story Case Base Is for Situations That Do Not Have a Clear-Cut Answer

When you are confused about what to do in a given situation, you want to ask for advice. But most people really don't want to hear the answers to their questions. They simply want to hear stories that deal with some of the same issues and use those stories as a guide. Sometimes they are happy to hear contradictory stories that make it clear there is no right answer, but nevertheless give them information to chew on when making a decision. A *situation advisor* attempts to understand the problem the user is having and then takes the stories from the database to dynamically create a panel of experts for every type of situation to be dealt with. These experts tell their stories and ask the user whether he or she is still confused and wants to hear more. It is a simple idea, a database of great decision-making stories tailored to specific situations, to be readied at the moment someone needs some words of wisdom.

Another situation involves the use of a collection of stories to construct networks of people who can be used as advisors in real time. In this use, the user describes the situation and the computer finds the most relevant stories in the database to help the user think about the problem. When the user finds one or more people to be especially helpful, he or she asks for the ability to converse online with the real-live version of these people. In this kind of database, the stories would come from people who have already agreed to be contacted in this way after some initial questions had been asked and after their most important stories had been heard. At that point the dialogue would continue face-or-face (or online). The value of this type of system is to cut out the initial questions that users might have that get the basics from an expert and put them in contact with the expert after they know enough to have a good conversation.

The real issue is this. People need help. They need help in doing their jobs and in living their lives. There are plenty of people around who can provide that help. But how exactly does that happen? You can't just call up an expert and ask her for advice. You might not know whom to call. The expert might not want to talk to you. You might not be ready to understand the advice that is offered. You might want to take the advice and not know how. You may not know you need advice. You may not know that the advice you need exists. Training, indeed all teaching, is about preparing someone to hear advice. It is about making him care about the story he is about to hear. And it is about making sure that there are good stories to hear. These stories can come from live people, prerecorded people, text on screen, or text from books. But will it be listened to? That is the question. A good training program makes sure that the advice is good and germane to the user. To really accomplish this the teacher, or the program that is doing the teaching, must be really smart.

Now is the time.

◊   ◊   ◊

Jump Start Your Thinking

To pique your interest in AI, here is some background:

People in business who are old enough remember when AI was going to take everyone's job away or make everyone's job easier or do something amazing or frightening. In the early Eighties every single national news magazine, it seemed, had major articles on robots, expert systems, or impressive abilities being exhibited by a computer. So what happened? Where are the intelligent computers?

One thing that happened was that AI was way over-hyped by the media. Of course, this wasn't entirely the media's fault.

Always on the lookout for cool stories about computers, it was easy enough to find AI researchers who were willing to promise the moon. Venture capitalists, always a sucker for something everyone else thinks is great and ready to leap on the bandwagon, funded AI companies by the fistful.

AI started out innocently enough. Smart people played chess, so it followed that computers that could play chess would be pretty smart. The U.S. Department of Defense figured that smart computers would lead to smart weapons, so money was available for chess-playing machines. Expert systems followed from those. If a machine could reason about chess playing, why not about oil drilling or medical diagnosis or chip design? Expertise is expertise, the reasoning went, so once you could get the rules that people followed in reasoning into a computer, computers would be able to do all sorts of things. This sounded plausible to all—generals, investment bankers, and AI researchers.

Some good results followed. But what passed in AI circles as a good result was a really good demo. From demo to product is a long road. It was hard to see what the product might be for the AI folks, so the venture capitalists had an answer: expert system shells.

At the time that all this was happening, in the early Eighties, AI was being worked on in just a handful of labs around the country, mostly at Stanford, Carnegie Mellon, and MIT. (I ran a small lab at Yale at this time.) There just weren't that many AI people around, so it was hard to see how they could hand code all the expert systems that anyone might want. Or to put this another way, venture capitalists didn't think they could make a lot of money in the custom software business. The expert system shell was a tool that allowed anyone at any company to build an expert system. Just put in the rules that describe the expertise you want to model, and voila, a smart computer with just the right expertise!

Well, that was how it was sold anyhow. Plenty of companies bought. They all wanted to be in the expert system business. They wanted to build smart machines. Unfortunately, this simple scheme was just that—a simple scheme. There was an art to modeling expertise and simply purchasing a shell didn't teach you that art. Further, expertise is most likely a lot more than a system of rules. Experts make mistakes, for example, and they remember them and they learn from them. There was no way for a system of rules to get smarter.

I pointed these things out at the time, but the media wanted positive stories not negative ones, and venture people figured they could make a lot of money from shells no matter what I thought. Eventually, defense department people soured on AI, because the business community said it didn't work, and suddenly there was no money and no more AI.

There is a lesson from all this that is useful for people in the world of training. Beware of people selling learning management systems. Those are the same venture capitalists with the same idea one more time. Let the companies do the work and convince them to buy the venture capitalists' tool despite the fact that it takes serious expertise to build a good e-learning system, just like it takes serious expertise to build an expert system. Caveat emptor.

AI is not dead. The ideas about intelligence and cognitive modeling on a computer are still around and there are folks working on newer and better ideas. When a good application area can be found, it is possible to use and expand on those ideas and make smart software in a given domain of expertise. Story databases are just one of a whole range of things that could be built.

Keep AI in mind when you think there is a problem that you need a smart computer to do. It may just be possible.

About the Author

Roger C. Schank became well-known in the early 1970s while an assistant professor at Stanford when he was the first to get computers to be able to process typewritten everyday English language sentences. His model for representing knowledge and the relationships between concepts, known as "Conceptual Dependency Theory," enabled his programs to predict what concepts might be coming next in a sentence.

Schank moved to Yale in 1974, where he built the first newspaper story-reading program for computers and became chairman of Yale's computer science department. In order to get computers to tie sentences together, Schank (working with Abelson), came up with the notion of a script to keep the inferences that computers made from exploding exponentially.

After turning his attention to learning, he created the theory of "Case-Based Reasoning" to deal with how people learn and reason from experience.

In 1989 he moved to Northwestern University, where he established the Institute for the Learning Sciences (ILS), whose premise was based on learning through simulation supported by just-in-time storytelling in a goal-based scenario. Hundreds of simulations were built for such clients as Andersen, EPA, the U.S. Army, and public schools.

To instantiate these ideas in online degree programs, Schank developed a much less costly version of his educational model, the "Story-Centered Curriculum," wherein one inhabits a fictional world analogous to real life. Schank moved to Carnegie Mellon's new West Coast Campus in 2001 to direct the master's program in computer science. The program curriculum consists entirely of projects. Students work in teams on one project at a time, mentored by experts.

Schank now runs Socratic Arts, a company dedicated to helping schools and companies build meaningful curricula online. He is the author of twenty-two books, the most recent of which is *Making Minds Less Well Educated Than Our Own*. The best-known are *Scripts, Plans, Goals, and Understanding, Dynamic Memory, Tell Me a Story, Engines for Education*, and *Designing World-Class e-Learning*. He was recognized by ASTD in 2000 for his "distinguished contributions to workplace learning."

Index

A

Abdelgwad, A., 168–169, 170
Academic training: Dragon Slaying parable on, 183–187, 189–191; similarities of corporate training departments and, 187–189, 252–253
Adams, H., 159
Advisory system, 204
AI (Artificial Intelligence): as answer to theory/technology question, 263–264; author's work with, 224; building story databases using, 273; growing interest in e-learning use of, 258–261; improving training systems through, 261–262; to jump start your thinking about using, 277–280; training applications of, 274–277; "When Philosophers Encounter AI" (Dennett) article on, 226–227
AI indexing problem: 1: description/overview of, 265–267; 2: of how to best retrieve the story, 267–271; 3: how to redirect the conversation, 271–272
AI Magazine, 259
AI problems: of getting right knowledge to user on time, 264–265; good teaching strategy as, 272–273; the indexing, 265–272

AI training applications: for adding expertise to training, 275; tremendous potential of, 274–275; for using story database to exploring issues, 275–276
Airport security: profiling by, 171; training by, 110–111, 115–116
"Alice's Restaurant" (Guthrie), 1
Andersen Consulting, 204
Anticipation, 213, 214
Assessment. *See* E-learning evaluation

B

Bartlett's memory research, 93–94
A Beautiful Mind (film), 162
Behavior: controlling rude behavior of employees, 85–87; dealing swiftly with bad, 88–89; do's and don't of teaching, 89–90; imprinting new nonconscious, 87; nonconscious teaching of, 83–85, 89; practicing desired, 87. *See also* Change; Stereotypes; Teaching
Beneficial stereotyping: determining how to build, 178–181; how to teach, 174–178; learning what to look for with customers as, 180; tools for teaching, 181–182
Beneficial stereotyping process:

concentrate on categories and features, 177–178; create rich mental images, 175–176; rely on stories to reflect experience, 176–177, 181–182

Beneficial stereotyping tools: 1: statistics, 181; 2: odds, 181; 3: stories, 181–182; 4: talking about stereotypes, 182; 5: predictions, 182

Blanc, G., 144

"The blended approach," 207, 248

Bocuse, P., 144

Bueller, F. (fictional character), 230, 233

C

CBT (computer-based training), 205, 209–210. *See also* E-learning

Change: challenges of teaching, 41; example of teaching, 42–44. *See also* Behavior

Chomsky, N., 226, 227

CMU West: article written on learning-by-doing class at, 219–221; "Day in the Life at CMU West" (Raygoza), 195–197; learning-by-doing project-based scenarios used at, 154–157; SCC (story centered curriculum) used at, 194–197, 218

Communication problems: e-learning failure to solve Enron's, 70–71; e-learning as supposed solution to Enron's, 69–70; Enron's, 60–69; finding real solution to teaching, 71–74

Communication skills: challenge of teaching, 71–76; practicing, 75–76; as training learning objective, 151–152

Community colleges, 140–141

COMMUNITY reward, 25, 29–30, 32–33, 34

Conversation: AI indexing problem and redirecting the, 271–272; as learning by doing, 16–17

Corporate Dragon Slaying training: evaluating your e-learning, 254–257; Novations catalog courses on, 241–251; using SCC as solution to, 253; similar problems faced by academic and, 187–189, 252–253; story on, 240–241

Creativity, 78

The Critique of Pure Reason (Kant), 159

Curriculum: application of SCC, 194–197; defining, 189; Dragon Slaying parable on, 183–187, 189–191, 240–257; examples of story-centered, 199–202; goals included in ideal, 189–191; how to build a SCC, 192–194; introducing SCC, 191; questions to ask about, 230–234; story told by good, 192; training program, 197–199. *See also* Teaching; Training

D

"Day in the Life at CMU West" (Raygoza), 195–197

Deloitte & Touche case study, 199–201

Dennett, D. C., 226

Dialogue for learning, 16–17

Doing-based training: corporate knowledge base as ignoring doing and, 150; difficulty of doing things on the web for,

153; difficulty in recreating real-life situations for, 153; feedback and reflection as part of, 145, 146; jump starting your thinking about, 159–160; sample scenario for, 154–157; sample step-by-step guide for, 157–158; top ten reasons why trainers fail to facilitate, 141–142; training department list of learning objectives without doing, 151–153; why trainers don't know how to facilitate, 142–146. *See also* Learning by doing

Doing-based training excuses: no experts available for practice situation, 150; real-life situation is too hard to replicate in classroom, 147–148; subject matter doesn't seem doing oriented, 146–147; takes too long to have trainees actually try things out, 148–149; we want to teach general principles, 158

Dragon Slaying: parable of academic education on, 183–187, 189–191; parable of corporate training on, 240–257; SCC (story-centered curriculum) created for, 192–194, 198–199

E

E-learning: basic elements of engagement for, 210–211; "the blended approach" using, 207, 248; considering origins of, 206–208; evaluating your training, 254–257; funkyfresh.com tips for, 216–217; improving training systems through AI, 261–262; Novations catalog courses on, 241–251; tips on

training using, 222–223; why it isn't fun, 205–208. *See also* CBT (computer-based training)

E-learning design: building elements of engagement into, 211–213; customer complaints about, 52; do's and don'ts on, 58–59; the right questions to ascertain learning needs for, 57; rules of thumb for building, 52–56; typical flaws in, 49–51; understanding that some things cannot be taught prior to, 57–58

E-learning engagement elements: anticipation, 213–214; emotional identification, 214–216; listed, 210, 211–212

E-learning evaluation: course catalog is too big, 254–257; the courses are too short, 255; the training is generic and one size fits all, 256–263; the word "blended" is being used, 255

E-learning flaws: 1: they involve telling and not doing, 49–50; 2: they use cleverness and not fun learning, 50; 3: lack of good storytelling, 50–51; 4: relentless use of quizzes, 51

E-learning problems: courses are too short, 255; using overly large catalogs for, 254–257; the training is generic, 256–257; the word "blended" is being used, 255

E-learning rules of thumb: considering why most training is so bad, 56; described and listed, 52–53; including the SME (subject matter experts), 53–55; try thinking about doing rather than knowing, 55–56

"E-speak" (Enron), 68
EGO reward, 25, 27
Eliot, C., 232–233
Emotional identification, 214–216. *See also* Feelings
Employees: do's and don't of teaching behavior to, 89–90; hiring the right, 86–87; practicing desired behavior, 87
Enron: communication problems of, 60–62, 68–69; e-learning as supposed communication solution for, 69–70; Enron perspectives on their communication issues, 62–64; failure of e-learning to solve communication problem at, 71; goal based scenario approach to examine communication at, 63–65; websites on communication problems of, 61, 66–68
EPA (U.S. Environmental Protection Agency), 66
ESD (Express for Software Development) [Deloitte & Touche], 199–201
Eskimo folk tale, 94
"An Essay Concerning Human Understanding" (Locke), 159
Euclid, 5
Euclidean geometry, 5
Event memory: birthday party menu experiment on, 91–93, 94–103; difference between procedural and, 105–108
Experts. *See* SME (subject matter experts)
EXTERNAL HOPE reward, 25, 28
EXTERNAL reward, 26, 31

F
Feedback, 145, 146
Feelings: as part of stereotyping

process, 174; role in memory, 103–104. *See also* Emotional identification
Ferris Bueller's Day Off (film), 230
Fodor, J., 226, 227
Fun: defining, 209; learning as, 208–210; tips on making e-learning, 222–223; why e-learning isn't, 205–208
funkyfresh.com, 216–217

G
Goal based scenario approach: benefits of using, 65–66; computer simulations using, 63; Enron communication problems examined using, 64–65; "A Matter of Meetings," 64–65
Goals: included in ideal curriculum, 189–191; learning is best when in pursuit of, 231; naturally occurring, 33–37. *See also* Learning
Google.com, 224, 229
Guthrie, A., 1

H
HABIT reward, 25, 26–27
Handling Customer Complaints training course, 3
Hartman, J., 168–170
Hernández, D., 168
HOPE (external) reward, 25, 28
HOPE (internal) reward, 25, 29

I
IBM, 256
ILS (Institute for the Learning Sciences), 204, 258
Imprinting new nonconscious behaviors, 87
INTERNAL HOPE reward, 25, 29
INTERNAL reward, 26, 32, 33, 34

K

Kant, I., 159
Kaufman, Herr, 144–146
Knowledge: classic AI problem of matching user to right, 264–265; procedural, 11, 107–108; recall, 11–12
KNOWLEDGE reward, 25, 30, 33, 34

L

Lay, K., 66, 67
Learning: asking the right questions to ascertain needs of, 57; "the blended approach" to, 207; dialogue for, 16–17; fallacy of reward systems for, 20–21; questions to ask on, 230–234; real motivation for, 23–24; storytelling as heart of understanding and, 217; trainee rewards for, 25–33, 34–35; typically true items about natural, 33–34. *See also* Goals; Naturally occurring learning goals; Teaching
Learning by doing: described, 12–13, 141; example of chef and, 144–146; feedback and reflection as part of, 145, 146; jump starting your thinking about, 159–160; practice as part of, 13–16, 19, 145–146; Socratic teaching linked to, 148; time constraints as enemy of, 149; top ten reasons why trainers fail to facilitate, 141–142; training approached as, 153–158; why trainers don't know how to facilitate, 142–146. *See also* Doing-based training
Learning objectives: described, 151; students to identify con-structive/destructive relationship elements, 152; students to identify effective communication skills, 151–152; as trivializing complex issues, 152; try not making lists of training, 152–153
LIBITI (Learn it because I thought it!), 5–7
Locke, J., 159
Lung cancer lab simulations, 115

M

"A Matter of Meetings" (goal based scenario), 64–65
Memory: Bartlett's research on, 93–94; birthday party menu experiment on, 91–93, 94–103; difference between event and procedural, 105–108; role of feelings/behaviors of others in, 103–104; stereotyping from common images in our, 172
Mentors: characteristics of good, 18–19; online mentoring by, 154. *See also* Trainers
Mexican troops stereotype, 164–165, 166
Michelin Guides, 143
Minsky, M., 227
Monroe, J., 169
Motivation: how to teach desire for success and, 44–45; hypothetical trainee, 22; using naturally occurring learning goals/rewards for, 35; real trainee learning, 23–24

N

Naturally occurring learning goals: 1: making sure training is group process, 35–36; 2: make sure training is problem-solving process, 36; 3: make sure that whatever is learned is merely a prelude, 37; 4: make sure independence is in sight, 38; to facilitate motivation, 35; tope ten list of truisms about, 33–34. *See also* Learning

The New York Times, 168

Novations training catalog: assessment and report on, 250–251; Conflict Management, 241; Customer Service Teamwork, 242–244; Dilemmas of Internal Customer Service, 242; End User Courses, 243-244; Handling Violence in the Workplace, 242; Handling Workplace Conflict(Employee Version), 242; Handling Workplace Conflict (Manager Version), 242; Keeping Customer Service Skills Strong, 242; Leading Customer Service Teams, 242; Technical Courses, 243–244; Understanding Customer Loyalty, 242

O

Oracle Corporation case study, 201–202

Organizational culture: "standards" story representing, 128–130; storytelling encouraged by, 128–130

P

Peggy Sue Got Married (film), 21

Plato, 141, 160

Practice/practicing: of communication skills, 75–76; of desired behavior, 87, 88–89; encouraged by good mentors, 19; using goal-based scenarios for, 66; learning by doing through,
13–16, 19, 145–146; no experts available for one-on-one, 150; procedural memory and, 106–107; time constraints as enemy of, 149; what is impossible to practice, 112–113

Pretty Woman (film), 167

PROBLEM SOLVING reward, 25, 28–29, 32, 34

Procedural knowledge: described, 11; fallacy of classroom training in, 107–108

Procedural memory: difference between event and, 105–108; role of practice in, 106–107

Profiling, 171. *See also* Stereotypes

Q

QUALIFICATIONS reward, 25–26, 30–31, 33, 34

Questions: asking the right, 228–230; bad training, 238–239; on creating high-performance individuals, 234–236; Eliot's list of teaching, 232–233; good training, 3, 239; on how people learn/what they need to learn, 230–234; jump starting your training using, 238–239; relevance of AI answer to theory/technology, 263–264; timely context of good, 230; when to disagree with the, 236–238. *See also* Training

R

Racquetball strategy, 178–179

Racquetball theory of life, 161–163, 180–181

Raygoza, M., 195

Recall knowledge, 11–12

Recognition knowledge, 11

Reflection, 145, 146

Reward systems: behavior reinforcement using, 88–89; fallacy of training, 20–21; training for things never encountered by changing, 117–119

Roberts, J., 167

Russell, B., 159

S

Saleh, T., 43–44

SCC (story centered curriculum): described, 192; how it works, 194–197; how to build a, 192–194; introducing, 191; as solution to corporate Dragon Slaying training, 253; training programs using, 197–199; two examples of, 199–202

Schank, R., 226–227

School-like questions, 237, 238

September 11th, 116

Simulations: AI potential for facilitating, 275; built at ILS, 258; difficulties with using, 12–13; goal based scenario approach used in, 63; growing appreciation in value of, 260; lung cancer lab, 115; need for reality feeling, 253

Situation advisor, 276

SME (subject matter experts): AI potential for facilitating, 275; cornerstone role in process of training design, 56; getting taped interviews of, 150; included in e-learning design, 53–55; unavailable to one-on-one practice help, 150

Socrates, 17

Socratic Arts, 199, 201

Socratic teaching: characteristics of trainer who uses, 17–19;

learning by doing linked to, 148

Spinoza, B., 160

Stereotypes: determining how to beneficially build, 178–181; examined by using Mexican troops news item, 164–165, 166; examining how we, 172–174; examining pros and cons of, 164–167; how to teach beneficial, 174–178; problem with misleading, 166; public interactions based on, 163; racquetball strategy and, 178–179; racquetball theory of life on, 161–163, 180–181; teaching people to not make, 167–172; tools for teaching beneficial, 181–182. *See also* Behavior; Profiling

Stereotyping process: 1: we rely on common images from memory, 172; 2: we remember prior cases, 172–173; 3: we form categories, 173; 4: we remember exceptions, 173; 5: we get a feeling, 174; 6: we miss the forest for the trees, 174

Stereotyping well. *See* Beneficial stereotyping

Stories: AI indexing problem of redirecting conversation of, 271–272; AI indexing problem of retrieving, 267–271; using AI to build databases of, 273; growing appreciation in value of, 260; for situations without clear-cut answers, 275–276; tips on using training, 130–139; told during training, 124–125; which change focus to what the trainee needs, 273

Storytelling: basics of, 127; beneficial stereotyping through experience and, 176–177, 181–182; Dragon Slaying parable, 183–187, 189–191; e-learning lack of good, 50–51; encouraged by organizational culture, 128–130; examining beliefs in, 125–128; example of official, 124–125; funkyfresh.com tips for, 216–217; as heart of understanding and learning, 217; "standards," 128–130; value of good, 121–124

Storytelling tips: include "story choice" as part of the story, 134; listed, 130; make sure tellers are authentic, 132–133; make sure tellers don't blandify the story, 133; never tell without using a story, 131–132; use real stories, 130–131; recognize that story living is better than storytelling, 136–137; remember Billy's story, 138; surprise your listener, 137; tell only those stories that can be heard, 135; tell stories just in time, 135–136; things to think about when hearing a story, 138–139; things to think about when telling a story, 139

Success/motivation teaching, 44–45

T

Teaching: AI problem of using good strategies of, 272–273; challenge of communication skills, 71–76; challenges of teaching change, 41–44; to create high-performance individuals, 234–236; differences between what can/cannot be taught, 76–79, 80; how to stereotype well, 174–178; how to teach courtesy/handling of difficult situations, 85–87; how to teach motivation to succeed, 44–45; and knowing what cannot be taught, 46, 57–58; nonconscious, 83–85, 89; people to not make stereotypes, 167–172; tools for beneficial stereotyping, 181–182; why trainers don't know how to teach by doing, 142–146. *See also* Behavior; Curriculum; Learning; Training

Telling principles: 1: don't tell people thing that they cannot immediately make use of, 7; 2: don't tell people how to do something they will never have to actually do, 7–8; 3: don't make me guess the right answer, 9–10; 4: it doesn't really matter what you can show that you know, 10–12; 5: have somebody do something, 12–13; 6: if you teach it have them practice it, 13–16; 7: using dialogue for learning, 16–17

Tocqueville, A. de, 159

Trainee learning rewards: 1: HABIT, 25, 26–27; 2: EGO, 25, 27; 3: HOPE (external), 25, 28; 4: PROBLEM SOLVING, 25, 28–29, 32, 34; 5: HOPE (internal), 25, 29; 6: COMMUNITY, 25, 29–30, 32–33, 34; 7: KNOWLEDGE, 25, 30, 33, 34; 8: QUALIFICATIONS, 25–26, 30–31, 33, 34; 9: EXTERNAL, 26, 31; 10: INTERNAL, 26, 32, 33, 34; a few reminders about, 38–39;

learning role of, 34–35; listed, 25–26; short list for, 32–33

Trainees: classic AI problem of matching right knowledge to, 264–265; difficulties in actually trying things out by, 148–149; hypothetical motivations for doing well by, 22; real motivation for learning by, 23–24; rewards inherent in reasons for wanting to do well by, 25–32; stories which change focus to needs of, 273

Trainers: characteristics of Socratic, 17–19; perception of all problems as training problems by, 70–71; top ten reasons for failure to teach by doing, 141–142; why they don't know how to teach by doing, 142–146. *See also* Mentors

Training: AI applications to, 274–277; approached as learning by doing, 153–158; determining what is appropriate for, 76–79; differences between real life and, 73–74; Dragon Slaying parable on, 183–187, 189–191, 240–257; how to stereotype well, 174–178; improving through use of AI, 261–262; people to not make stereotypes in business, 167–172; perceived as solution to all problems, 70–71; pointers on jump starting your, 46–47; questions about, 3; role of feelings in memory of, 103–104; someone for something which may never happen, 111–112; storytelling told during, 124–128, 130–139; telling principles in context of, 7–17; what memory experiments tells us about, 104–105.

See also Curriculum; Questions; Teaching

Training departments: Dragon Slaying parable on, 183–187, 189–191, 240–257; learning objectives of, 151–153; Novations catalog courses offered by, 241–251; resemblance between academic schools and, 187–189

Training design: challenge of creating high quality but inexpensive, 262–263; curriculum portion of, 197–199; example of not considering learners in, 3–4; LIBITI problem with, 5–7; rules of thumb for the, 33–34

Training programs: do's and don't of teaching behavior in, 89–90; learning objectives of, 151–153; SCC (story centered curriculum), 192–202; teaching employees courtesy/to handle difficult situations, 85–87

Training undone by reality problem: 1: stop training people for things they will never do, 114–116; 2: train people by kindling deep emotional reactions, 116–117; 3: train people by changing the reward system, 117–119; do's and don'ts of, 119–120

U

U.S. Environmental Protection Agency, 66

V

Vietnam War, 179

W

Wachovia, 256

Wal-Mart, 57
Websites: on Dragon Slaying parable, 189–191; on e-learning courses, 248–249; on Enron communication problems, 61, 66–68; funkyfresh.com, 216–217; Google.com to search, 224, 229

"West Coast Campus Celebrates First Graduating Class," 219–221
"When Philosophers Encounter AI" (Dennett), 226–227
Wilde, O., 160
Winograd, T., 226
Wong, P.T.P., 61

Pfeiffer Publications Guide

This guide is designed to familiarize you with the various types of Pfeiffer publications. The formats section describes the various types of products that we publish; the methodologies section describes the many different ways that content might be provided within a product. We also provide a list of the topic areas in which we publish.

FORMATS

In addition to its extensive book-publishing program, Pfeiffer offers content in an array of formats, from fieldbooks for the practitioner to complete, ready-to-use training packages that support group learning.

FIELDBOOK Designed to provide information and guidance to practitioners in the midst of action. Most fieldbooks are companions to another, sometimes earlier, work, from which its ideas are derived; the fieldbook makes practical what was theoretical in the original text. Fieldbooks can certainly be read from cover to cover. More likely, though, you'll find yourself bouncing around following a particular theme, or dipping in as the mood, and the situation, dictate.

HANDBOOK A contributed volume of work on a single topic, comprising an eclectic mix of ideas, case studies, and best practices sourced by practitioners and experts in the field.

An editor or team of editors usually is appointed to seek out contributors and to evaluate content for relevance to the topic. Think of a handbook not as a ready-to-eat meal, but as a cookbook of ingredients that enables you to create the most fitting experience for the occasion.

RESOURCE Materials designed to support group learning. They come in many forms: a complete, ready-to-use exercise (such as a game); a comprehensive resource on one topic (such as conflict management) containing a variety of methods and approaches; or a collection of like-minded activities (such as icebreakers) on multiple subjects and situations.

TRAINING PACKAGE An entire, ready-to-use learning program that focuses on a particular topic or skill. All packages comprise a guide for the facilitator/trainer and a workbook for the participants. Some packages are supported with additional media—such as video—or learning aids, instruments, or other devices to help participants understand concepts or practice and develop skills.

- *Facilitator/trainer's guide* Contains an introduction to the program, advice on how to organize and facilitate the learning event, and step-by-step instructor notes. The guide also contains copies of presentation materials—handouts, presentations, and overhead designs, for example—used in the program.

- *Participant's workbook* Contains exercises and reading materials that support the learning goal and serves as a valuable reference and support guide for participants in the weeks and months that follow the learning event. Typically, each participant will require his or her own workbook.

ELECTRONIC CD-ROMs and web-based products transform static Pfeiffer content into dynamic, interactive experiences. Designed to take advantage of the searchability, automation, and ease-of-use that technology provides, our e-products bring convenience and immediate accessibility to your workspace.

METHODOLOGIES

CASE STUDY A presentation, in narrative form, of an actual event that has occurred inside an organization. Case studies are not prescriptive, nor are they used to prove a point; they are designed to develop critical analysis and decision-making skills. A case study has a specific time frame, specifies a sequence of events, is narrative in structure, and contains a plot structure—an issue (what should be/have been done?). Use case studies when the goal is to enable participants to apply previously learned theories to the circumstances in the case, decide what is pertinent, identify the real issues, decide what should have been done, and develop a plan of action.

ENERGIZER A short activity that develops readiness for the next session or learning event. Energizers are most commonly used after a break or lunch to stimulate or refocus the group. Many involve some form of physical activity, so they are a useful way to counter post-lunch lethargy. Other uses include transitioning from one topic to another, where "mental" distancing is important.

EXPERIENTIAL LEARNING ACTIVITY (ELA) A facilitator-led intervention that moves participants through the learning cycle from experience to application (also known as a Structured Experience). ELAs are carefully thought-out designs in which there is a definite learning purpose and intended outcome. Each step—everything that participants do during the activity—facilitates the accomplishment of the stated goal. Each ELA includes complete instructions for facilitating the intervention and a clear statement of goals, suggested group size and timing, materials required, an explanation of the process, and, where appropriate, possible variations to the activity. (For more detail on Experiential Learning Activities, see the Introduction to the *Reference Guide to Handbooks and Annuals*, 1999 edition, Pfeiffer, San Francisco.)

GAME A group activity that has the purpose of fostering team spirit and togetherness in addition to the achievement of a pre-stated goal. Usually contrived—undertaking a desert expedition, for example—this type of learning method offers an engaging means for participants to demonstrate and practice business and interpersonal skills. Games are effective for team building and personal development mainly because the goal is subordinate to the process—the means through which participants reach decisions, collaborate, communicate, and generate trust and understanding. Games often engage teams in "friendly" competition.

ICEBREAKER A (usually) short activity designed to help participants overcome initial anxiety in a training session and/or to acquaint the participants with one another. An icebreaker can be a fun activity or can be tied to specific topics or training goals. While a useful tool in itself, the icebreaker comes into its own in situations where tension or resistance exists within a group.

INSTRUMENT A device used to assess, appraise, evaluate, describe, classify, and summarize various aspects of human behavior. The term used to describe an instrument depends primarily on its format and purpose. These terms include survey, questionnaire, inventory, diagnostic, survey, and poll. Some uses of instruments include providing instrumental feedback to group members, studying here-and-now processes or functioning within a group, manipulating group composition, and evaluating outcomes of training and other interventions.

Instruments are popular in the training and HR field because, in general, more growth can occur if an individual is provided with a method for focusing specifically on his or her own behavior. Instruments also are used to obtain information that will serve as a basis for change and to assist in workforce planning efforts.

Paper-and-pencil tests still dominate the instrument landscape with a typical package comprising a facilitator's guide, which offers advice on administering the instrument and interpreting the collected data, and an initial set of instruments. Additional instruments are available separately. Pfeiffer, though, is investing heavily in e-instruments. Electronic instrumentation provides effortless distribution and, for larger groups particularly, offers advantages over paper-and-pencil tests in the time it takes to analyze data and provide feedback.

LECTURETTE A short talk that provides an explanation of a principle, model, or process that is pertinent to the participants' current learning needs. A lecturette is intended to establish a common language bond between the trainer and the participants by providing a mutual frame of reference. Use a lecturette as an introduction to a group activity or event, as an interjection during an event, or as a handout.

MODEL A graphic depiction of a system or process and the relationship among its elements. Models provide a frame of reference and something more tangible, and more easily remembered, than a verbal explanation. They also give participants something to "go on," enabling them to track their own progress as they experience the dynamics, processes, and relationships being depicted in the model.

ROLE PLAY A technique in which people assume a role in a situation/ scenario: a customer service rep in an angry-customer exchange, for example. The way in which the role is approached is then discussed and feedback is offered. The role play is often repeated using a different approach and/or incorporating changes made based on feedback received. In other words, role playing is a spontaneous interaction involving realistic behavior under artificial (and safe) conditions.

SIMULATION A methodology for understanding the interrelationships among components of a system or process. Simulations differ from games in that they test or use a model that depicts or mirrors some aspect of reality in form, if not necessarily in content. Learning occurs by studying the effects of change on one or more factors of the model. Simulations are commonly used to test hypotheses about what happens in a system—often referred to as "what if?" analysis—or to examine best-case/worst-case scenarios.

THEORY A presentation of an idea from a conjectural perspective. Theories are useful because they encourage us to examine behavior and phenomena through a different lens.

TOPICS

The twin goals of providing effective and practical solutions for workforce training and organization development and meeting the educational needs of training and human resource professionals shape Pfeiffer's publishing program. Core topics include the following:

Leadership & Management

Communication & Presentation

Coaching & Mentoring

Training & Development

E-Learning

Teams & Collaboration

OD & Strategic Planning

Human Resources

Consulting

What will you find on pfeiffer.com?

- The best in workplace performance solutions for training and HR professionals

- Downloadable training tools, exercises, and content

- Web-exclusive offers

- Training tips, articles, and news

- Seamless on-line ordering

- Author guidelines, information on becoming a Pfeiffer Affiliate, and much more

Discover more at www.pfeiffer.com